Name ________________________________ Class ______________ Date __

Concept Review

Section: Energy Transfer

Complete each statement below by choosing a term from the following list. Use each term only once.

intensive	enthalpy	heat	higher
extensive	temperature	physical	lower

1. Temperature and heat are different but related ________________ properties.

2. If a sample has a(n) ________________ temperature than its surroundings, energy is transferred from the sample. If the temperature of the sample is ________________ than its surroundings, energy is transferred to the sample. The energy transferred between objects that are at different temperatures is ________________. The ________________ of a sample is a measure of the average kinetic energy of the particles in a sample.

3. The temperature of a sample does not depend on the amount of the sample, therefore temperature is a(n) ________________ property. In contrast, heat is a(n) ________________ property, which means that the amount of energy transferred as heat depends on the amount of the sample.

4. The total energy content of a sample is its ________________, and is represented by the symbol H.

Complete each statement below by writing the correct term in the space provided.

5. The SI temperature unit is ________________.

6. A kelvin is the same temperature interval as a degree ________________.

7. Because 0.00°C is equal to ________________, individual temperatures have different numerical values on the two scales.

8. A temperature difference taken between two objects has ________________ numerical value in Kelvins and in degrees Celsius.

9. Heat, like other forms of energy, is measured in ________________.

Concept Review *continued*

10. If the temperature of an object is found to be 73.15 K, its value in degrees

Celsius is _________________.

11. Kelvin temperature = Celsius temperature + _________________

Solve the following problems and write your answers in the space provided.

12. Calculate the energy needed to raise the temperature of 180.0 g of water from 10.0°C to 40.0°C. The molar heat capacity for water is 75.3 J/K·mol.

13. How many joules would be required to change the temperature of 250.0 g of aluminum from 15.0°C to 75.0°C? The molar heat capacity of aluminum is 24.2 J/K·mol.

14. How much energy is required to raise the temperature of 68.0 g of tin from 25.0°C to 80.0°C? The molar heat capacity of tin is 11.1 J/K·mol.

15. The molar heat capacity of nitrogen, N_2, is 29.1 J/K·mol. How much energy is required to raise the temperature of 40.5 g of nitrogen 45 K?

Skills Worksheet

Concept Review

Section: Using Enthalpy

Complete each statement below by writing the correct term in the space provided.

1. The total energy of a system is its _____________________,or H. The only

   way to measure energy is through a _____________________. The

   _____________________ enthalpy change is the enthalpy change of one

   mole of an element or compound.

2. When a pure substance is heated or cooled, but does not change state, the

   energy as heat is the _____________________ as the enthalpy change.

   Therefore the molar enthalpy change is equal to the _____________________

   _____________________ multiplied by the _____________________,or

   $\Delta H=$ _____________________.

3. A _____________________ enthalpy change means that the change requires

   energy and that the process is _____________________. A

   _____________________ enthalpy change means that the change releases

   energy or is a _____________________ process.

4. The science that examines the energy changes that accompany chemical and

   physical processes is called _____________________.

Solve the following problems and write your answers in the space provided.

5. How much does the molar enthalpy change when 147 g of water cools from
   90.0°C to 17.0°C? The molar heat capacity for water is 75.3 J/K·mol.

6. How much does the molar enthalpy change when 432 g of water is heated
   from 18.0°C to 71.0°C? The molar heat capacity for water is 75.3 J/K·mol.

Name _____________________________________ Class _________________ Date _____________

Concept Review

Section: Changes in Enthalpy During Chemical Reactions

Complete each statement below by writing the correct term in the space provided.

1. In most chemical reactions, the enthalpy change can be measured in terms of

   energy in the form of _____________________ released or gained during the

   reaction. A change in enthalpy in a reaction depends on many variables, but

   _____________________ is one of the most important. To standardize the

   enthalpies of reactions, data for _____________________ and

   _____________________ are presented at the standard thermodynamic

   temperature of _____________________ °C, or _____________________ K.

   When a chemical equation is used in calculating thermodynamic values,

   coefficients represent _____________________ of a substance. The enthalpy

   change in forming 1 mol of a substance from its elements at 298.15K is called

   the _____________________ of formation.

Write the answers to the following questions in the space provided.

2. Explain how the two types of calorimeters are used to measure the energy
   released or absorbed in a chemical reaction.

   ____

   ____

   ____

   ____

3. State Hess's law.

   ____

   ____

   ____

   ____

❚ Concept Review *continued*

Solve the following problems and write your answers in the space provided.

4. What is the enthalpy change for the following reaction? Is the reaction exothermic or endothermic?

$$Cl_2(g) + 2HBr(g) \rightarrow 2HCl(g) + Br_2(g)$$

5. What is the enthalpy change for the following reaction? Is the reaction exothermic or endothermic?

$$CaCO_3(s) \rightarrow CaO(s) + CO_2(g)$$

Name _________________________________ Class _______________ Date _____________

Concept Review

Section: Order and Spontaneity

Complete each statement below by writing the correct term in the space provided.

1. The property of a system that makes a process occur consists of two driving forces, a tendency toward the greatest _____________________ state and a tendency toward the lowest _____________________ state.

2. The quantity of entropy possessed by 1 mol of a substance is called _____________________.

3. The symbol for standard entropy is _____________________ and the units used are _____________________, the same as for molar heat capacity.

4. The thermodynamic quantity used to predict whether a reaction will occur spontaneously is _____________________ and is defined by the equation $G = $ _____________________.

Complete each statement below by writing the correct term in the space provided.

5. A reaction is more likely to occur if the change in entropy is _____________________.

6. The entropy of a substance _____________________ with temperature.

7. _____________________ have greater standard entropies than liquids.

8. _____________________ have the most freedom to move, so their standard entropies are the greatest.

9. At _____________________, no disorder means no entropy.

10. The entropy change of a reaction is standard entropy of the _____________________ minus the standard entropy of the _____________________.

11. Because the atoms in a diamond are in a more ordered state than in graphite, the change in entropy in changing graphite into a diamond is _____________________.

Concept Review *continued*

12. A system with more energy has more ________________.

13. A process is spontaneous if ΔG is ________________.

14. All spontaneous processes occur with a ________________ in Gibbs energy.

Complete each statement below by underlining the correct word or phrase in brackets. Refer to the following two expressions when answering the items below.

ΔH = enthalpy of products − enthalpy of reactants

$\Delta G = \Delta H - T\Delta S$

15. The products of an [endothermic, exothermic] reaction have an energy higher than that of the reactants.

16. In endothermic reactions, ΔH has a [positive, negative] value.

17. The drive to achieve a state of [minimum, maximum] Gibbs energy may be interpreted as the driving force of a chemical reaction.

18. A chemical reaction occurs if it is accompanied by a(n) [increase, decrease] in Gibbs energy.

19. If ΔG is negative, $-\Delta G$, the reaction is [spontaneous, nonspontaneous].

20. The expression for ΔG shows that when ΔH is negative and ΔS is positive, ΔG is [positive, negative]. Thus, [endothermic, exothermic] reactions, which are accompanied by a(n) [increase, decrease] in entropy of the system, are probable.

21. The expression for ΔG shows that when ΔH is positive and ΔS is negative, ΔG is [positive, negative]. This means that [endothermic, exothermic] reactions accompanied by a(n) [increase, decrease] in entropy are improbable.

22. At very high temperatures, the sign and magnitude of ΔG and the spontaneity of a reaction are determined primarily by the change in [enthalpy, entropy].

23. According to the expression for ΔG, the [higher, lower] the temperature for a positive entropy change, the greater the chances are that the reaction will be spontaneous.

24. When the temperature of a system is low, the product $T\Delta S$ is very [small, large] compared to the ΔH term and has little influence on the value of ΔG. In such cases, the reaction may occur as the [enthalpy, entropy] change predicts.

Solve the following problems and write your answers in the space provided.

25. What is the entropy change for the following reaction?

$$Ca(s) + 2H_2O(l) \rightarrow Ca(OH)_2(s) + H_2(g)$$

❙ Concept Review *continued*

26. What is the entropy change for the following reaction?

$$4HBr(g) + O_2(g) \rightarrow 2H_2O(l) + 2Br_2(l)$$

27. Calculate the change in Gibbs energy for the following reaction at 25°C. Is the reaction spontaneous?

$$2H_2O_2(l) \rightarrow 2H_2O(l) + O_2(g)$$

28. Calculate the change in Gibbs energy for the given reaction at 25°C. Is the reaction spontaneous?

$$CaCO_3(s) \rightarrow CaO(s) + CO_2(g)$$

Problem Solving

Thermochemistry

Thermochemistry deals with the changes in heat energy that accompany a chemical reaction. Heat energy is measured in a quantity called *enthalpy*, represented as H. The change in heat energy that accompanies a chemical reaction is represented as ΔH. Hess's law provides a method for calculating the ΔH of a reaction from tabulated data. This law states that if two or more chemical equations are added, the ΔH of the individual equations may also be added to find the ΔH of the final equation. As an example of how this law operates, look at the three reactions below.

(1)	$2H_2(g) + O_2(g) \rightarrow 2H_2O(l)$	$\Delta H = -571.6$ kJ/mol
(2)	$2H_2O_2(l) \rightarrow 2H_2(g) + 2O_2(g)$	$\Delta H = +375.6$ kJ/mol
(3)	$2H_2O_2(l) \rightarrow 2H_2O(l) + O_2(g)$	$\Delta H = ?$ kJ/mol

When adding equations 1 and 2, the 2 mol of $H_2(g)$ will cancel each other out, while only 1 mol of $O_2(g)$ will cancel.

$$2H_2(g) + O_2(g) \rightarrow 2H_2O(l)$$

$$2H_2O_2(l) \rightarrow 2H_2(g) + \tfrac{1}{2}O_2(g)$$

Combining what is left yields the following equation.

$$2H_2O_2(l) \rightarrow 2H_2O(l) + O_2(g)$$

Notice that this is the same equation as the third equation shown above. Adding the two ΔH values for the reactions 1 and 2 gives the ΔH value for reaction 3. Using Hess's law to calculate the enthalpy of this reaction, the following answer is obtained.

$$-571.6 \text{ kJ/mol} + 375.6 \text{ kJ/mol} = -196.0 \text{ kJ/mol}$$

Thus, the ΔH value for the reaction is -196.0 kJ/mol.

Equation 1 represents the formation of water from its elemental components. If equation 2 were written in reverse, it would represent the formation of hydrogen peroxide from its elemental components. Therefore, adding equations 1 and 2 is the equivalent of subtracting the equation for the formation of the reactants of equation 3 from the equation for the formation of the products of equation 3.

$$2H_2(g) + O_2(g) \rightarrow 2H_2O(l)$$
$$-[2H_2(g) + 2O_2(g) \rightarrow 2H_2O_2(l)]$$
$$2H_2O_2(l) \rightarrow 2H_2O(l) + O_2(g)$$

The enthalpy of the final reaction can be rewritten using the following equation.

$$\Delta H_{\text{reaction}} = \text{sum of } \Delta H^0_{f_{\text{products}}} - \text{sum of } \Delta H^0_{f_{\text{reactants}}}$$

The equation states that the enthalpy change of a reaction is equal to the sum of the enthalpies of formation of the products minus the sum of the enthalpies of formation of the reactants. This allows Hess's law to be extended to state that the

Problem Solving *continued*

enthalpy change of any reaction can be calculated by looking up the standard molar enthalpy of formation, ΔH_f^0, of each substance involved. Some common enthalpies of formation may be found in **Table 1.**

The enthalpy change, however, does not account for all of the energy change of a reaction. Changes in the disorder (entropy) of a system can add to or detract from the energy involved in the enthalpy change. This amount of energy is given by the expression $T\Delta S$, where T is the Kelvin temperature and ΔS is the change in entropy during the reaction. A large increase in entropy, such as when a gas is produced from a reaction of liquids or solids, can contribute significantly to the overall energy change. The total amount of energy available from a reaction is called *free energy* and is denoted by ΔG. Free energy is given by the following equation.

$$\Delta G_{reaction} = \Delta H_{reaction} - T\Delta S_{reaction}$$

TABLE 1 STANDARD ENTHALPIES OF FORMATION

Substance	ΔH_f^0 (kJ/mol)	Substance	ΔH_f^0 (kJ/mol)
$NH_3(g)$	−45.9	$HF(g)$	−273.3
$NH_4Cl(s)$	−314.4	$H_2O(g)$	−241.82
$NH_4F(s)$	−125	$H_2O(l)$	−285.8
$NH_4NO_3(s)$	−365.56	$H_2O_2(l)$	−187.8
$Br_2(l)$	0.00	$H_2SO_4(l)$	−813.989
$CaCO_3(s)$	−1207.6	$FeO(s)$	−825.5
$CaO(s)$	−634.9	$Fe_2O_3(s)$	−1118.4
$CH_4(g)$	−74.9	$MnO_2(s)$	−520.0
$C_3H_8(g)$	−104.7	$N_2O(g)$	+82.1
$CO_2(g)$	−393.5	$O_2(g)$	0.00
$F_2(g)$	0.00	$Na_2O(s)$	−414.2
$H_2(g)$	0.00	$Na_2SO_3(s)$	−1101
$HBr(g)$	−36.29	$SO_2(g)$	−296.8
$HCl(g)$	−92.3	$SO_3(g)$	−395.7

Problem Solving *continued*

General Plan for Solving Thermochemistry Problems

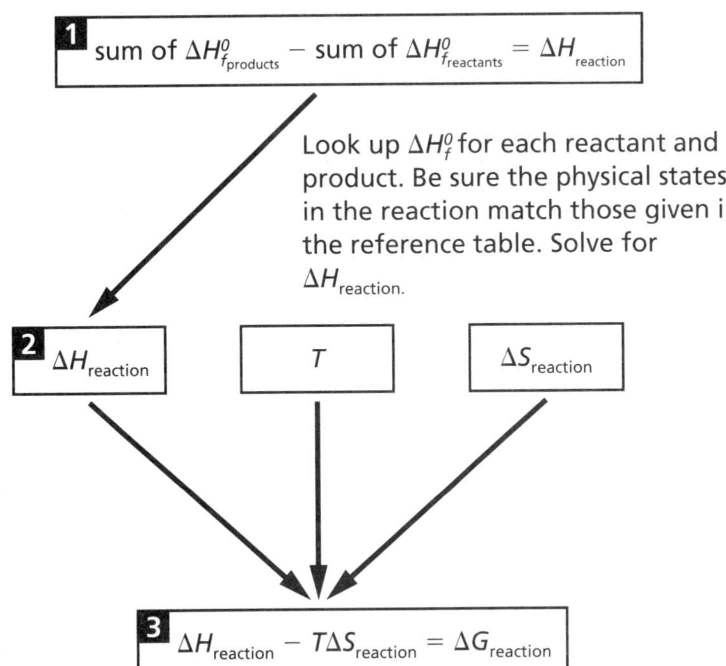

| Problem Solving *continued*

Sample Problem 1

Given the following two reactions and enthalpy data, calculate the enthalpy change for the reaction in which methane and oxygen combine to form ketene, CH_2CO, and water.

$$CH_2CO(g) + 2O_2(g) \rightarrow 2CO_2(g) + H_2O(g) \qquad \Delta H = -981.1 \text{ kJ}$$
$$CH_4(g) + 2O_2(g) \rightarrow CO_2(g) + 2H_2O(g) \qquad \Delta H = -802.3 \text{ kJ}$$

Solution

ANALYZE

What is given in the problem?   the desired product, chemical equations that can be added to obtain the desired product, and enthalpy changes for these chemical equations

What are you asked to find?   enthalpy change for the reaction in which methane and oxygen combine to form ketene and water

Items	Data
ΔH for reaction 1	-981.1 kJ
ΔH for reaction 2	-802.3 kJ

PLAN

What steps are needed to calculate ΔH for the reaction between methane and oxygen to form CH_2CO?

First, the two equations must be added to produce the final reaction. The first equation must be reversed so that ketene is a product, as shown in the final equation. The second equation must be multiplied by 2 so that carbon dioxide cancels out of the final equation. Then the individual enthalpies for the reactions must be added, adjusting for the fact that equation 1 is reversed and equation 2 is doubled.

$$2CO_2(g) + H_2O(g) \rightarrow CH_2CO(g) + 2O_2(g)$$
$$\underline{2 \times [CH_4(g) + 2O_2(g) \rightarrow CO_2(g) + 2H_2O(g)]}$$
$$2CH_4(g) + 2O_2(g) \rightarrow CH_2CO(g) + 3H_2O(g)$$

$$-\Delta H_{\text{reaction 1}}$$
$$\underline{+(2 \times \Delta H_{\text{reaction 2}})}$$
$$\Delta H_{\text{final reaction}}$$

Problem Solving *continued*

COMPUTE

$$2CO_2(g) + H_2O(g) \rightarrow CH_2CO(g) + 2O_2(g)$$
$$2CH_4(g) + 4O_2(g) \rightarrow 2CO_2(g) + 4H_2O(g)$$

$$2CO_2(g) + H_2O(g) + 2CH_4(g) + \overset{2}{\cancel{4}}O_2(g) \rightarrow$$
$$CH_2CO(g) + 2O_2(g) + 2CO_2(g) + \overset{3}{\cancel{4}}H_2O(g)$$

$$2CH_4(g) + 2O_2(g) \rightarrow CH_2CO(g) + 3H_2O(g)$$

$$-(-981.1 \text{ kJ})$$
$$+(2 \times -802.3 \text{ kJ})$$
$$\overline{-623.5 \text{ kJ}}$$

EVALUATE

Are the units correct?
Yes; adding terms in kilojoules gives an answer in kilojoules.

Is the number of significant figures correct?
Yes; the significant figures are correct. Rules for adding and rounding measurements give a result to four significant figures.

Is the answer reasonable?
Yes; the result can be approximated as -1600 kJ $+$ 1000 kJ $= -600$ kJ.

Practice

1. Calculate the reaction enthalpy for the following reaction.

$$5CO_2(g) + Si_3N_4(s) \rightarrow 3SiO(s) + 2N_2O(g) + 5CO(g)$$

Use the following equations and data.

$$(1) \quad CO(g) + SiO_2(s) \rightarrow SiO(g) + CO_2(g)$$
$$(2) \quad 8CO_2(g) + Si_3N_4(s) \rightarrow 3SiO_2(s) + 2N_2O(g) + 8CO(g)$$

$\Delta H_{\text{reaction 1}} = +520.9$ kJ
$\Delta H_{\text{reaction 2}} = +461.05$ kJ **ans: 2024 kJ**

Sample Problem 2

Calculate the heat of reaction for the decomposition of hydrogen peroxide to water and oxygen gas according to the following equation.

$$H_2O_2(l) \rightarrow H_2O(l) + O_2(g)$$

Use Table 1 for the necessary heats of formation.

Solution

ANALYZE

What is given in the problem? **the equation for the decomposition of H_2O_2, heats of formation given in Table 1**

What are you asked to find? **heat of reaction for the decomposition of H_2O_2**

Items	Data
ΔH decomposition of $H_2O_2(l)$	? kJ/mol
$\Delta H_f^0\, H_2O_2(l)$	-187.8 kJ/mol*
$\Delta H_f^0\, O_2(g)$	0.00 kJ/mol**
$\Delta H_f^0\, H_2O(l)$	-285.8 kJ/mol*

* from Table 1
** any pure elemental substance has a ΔH_f^0 of zero

PLAN

What steps are needed to calculate ΔH for the decomposition reaction?
First, the equation must be balanced. Add up the heats of formation for the products. From this quantity, subtract the heat of formation for the reactant.

Balance the equation for the decomposition of hydrogen peroxide.

$$2H_2O_2(l) \rightarrow 2H_2O(l) + O_2(g)$$

1

$$\text{sum of } \Delta H^0_{f_{products}} - \text{sum of } \Delta H^0_{f_{reactants}} = \Delta H_{reaction}$$

look up ΔH_f^0 for each reactant and product, and solve

2

$$\Delta H_{reaction}$$

given in Table 1

$$\left(2\Delta H^0_{f_{H_2O}} + \Delta H^0_{f_{O_2}}\right) - \left(2\Delta H^0_{f_{H_2O_2}}\right) = \Delta H_{reaction}$$

COMPUTE

$$[2(-285.8 \text{ kJ/mol}) + 0.00 \text{ kJ/mol}] - [2(-187.8 \text{ kJ/mol})] = -196.0 \text{ kJ/mol}$$

❚ Problem Solving *continued*

EVALUATE

Are the units correct?
Yes; adding terms in kJ/mol gives kJ/mol.

Is the number of significant figures correct?
**Yes; rules for adding and rounding measurements give a result to four signifi-
cant figures.**

Is the answer reasonable?
Yes; the result can be approximated as −600 kJ/mol + 400 kJ/mol = −200 kJ/mol.

Practice

Determine ΔH for each of the following reactions.

1. The following reaction is used to make CaO from limestone.
$$CaCO_3(s) \rightarrow CaO(s) + CO_2(g) \quad \textbf{ans: 179.2 kJ/mol}$$

2. The following reaction represents the oxidation of FeO to Fe_2O_3.
$$2FeO(s) + O_2(g) \rightarrow Fe_2O_3(s) \quad \textbf{ans: 533 kJ/mol}$$

3. The following reaction of ammonia and hydrogen fluoride produces ammonium fluoride.
$$NH_3(g) + HF(g) \rightarrow NH_4F(s) \quad \textbf{ans: 194 kJ/mol}$$

Problem Solving *continued*

Sample Problem 3

Calculate the free-energy change for the following reaction at 25°C.

$$Ca(s) + 2H_2O(l) \rightarrow Ca(OH)_2(s) + H_2(g)$$

Use the following data.

$$\Delta H_{reaction} = -411.6 \text{ kJ/mol}; \Delta S_{reaction} = 31.8 \text{ J/mol}\cdot K$$

Solution

ANALYZE

What is given in the problem?   **T, ΔH, and ΔS for the reaction**

What are you asked to find?   **the free energy of the reaction, ΔG**

Items	Data
ΔH for the reaction at 25°C	-411.6 kJ/mol
ΔS for the reaction at 25°C	31.8 J/mol $\cdot$ K
Temperature	25°C = 298 K
ΔG for the reaction at 25°C	? kJ/mol

PLAN

What steps are needed to calculate ΔG for the given reaction?
Apply the relationship $\Delta G = \Delta H - T\Delta S$.

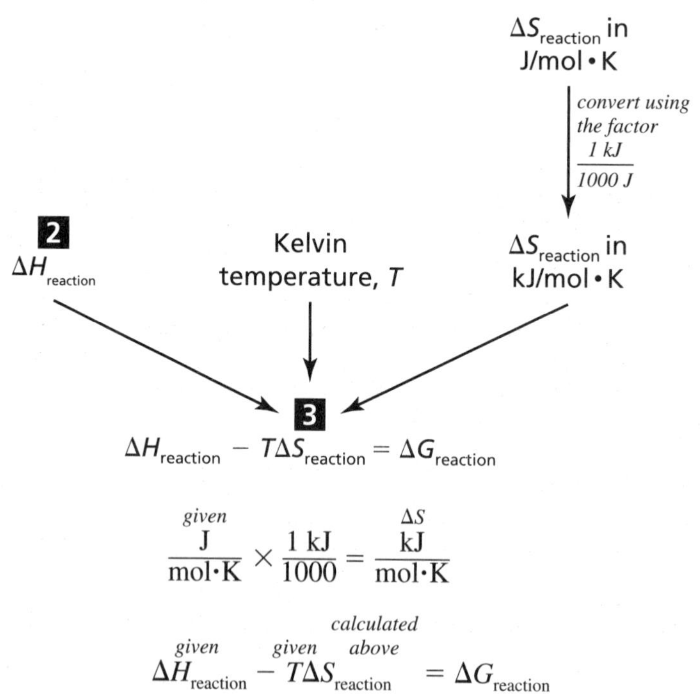

| **Problem Solving** *continued*

COMPUTE

$$\frac{31.8 \text{ J}}{\text{mol·K}} \times \frac{1 \text{ kJ}}{1000 \text{ J}} = 0.0318 \text{ kJ/mol·K}$$

$$-411.1 \text{ kJ/mol} - (298 \text{ K} \times 0.0318 \text{ kJ/mol·K}) = -411.6 \text{ kJ/mol} - 9.5 \text{ kJ/mol}$$

$$\Delta G_{\text{reaction}} = -421.1 \text{ kJ/mol}$$

Are the units correct?
Yes; the kelvin units canceled. Adding terms in kJ/mol gives kJ/mol.

Is the number of significant figures correct?
Yes; the number of significant figures is correct. Rules for adding and rounding measurements give a result with four significant figures.

Is the answer reasonable?
Yes; values were given for T, ΔH, and ΔS and the computation was carried out correctly.

Practice

1. Calculate the free energy change, ΔG, for the combustion of hydrogen sulfide according to the following chemical equation. Assume reactants and products are at 25°C.

$$H_2S(g) + O_2(g) \rightarrow H_2O(l) + SO_2(g)$$

$\Delta H_{\text{reaction}} = -562.1 \text{ kJ/mol}$
$\Delta S_{\text{reaction}} = -0.09278 \text{ kJ/mol·K}$ **ans: -534.5 kJ/mol**

2. Calculate the free energy change for the decomposition of sodium chlorate. Assume reactants and products are at 25°C.

$$NaClO_3(s) \rightarrow NaCl(s) + O_2(g)$$

$\Delta H_{\text{reaction}} = -19.1 \text{ kJ/mol}$
$\Delta S_{\text{reaction}} = 0.1768 \text{ kJ/mol·K}$ **ans: -71.8 kJ/mol**

3. Calculate the free energy change for the combustion of 1 mol of ethane. Assume reactants and products are at 25°C.

$$C_2H_6(g) + O_2(g) \rightarrow 2CO_2(g) + 3H_2O(l)$$

$\Delta H_{\text{reaction}} = -1561 \text{ kJ/mol}$
$\Delta S_{\text{reaction}} = 0.4084 \text{ kJ/mol·K}$ **ans: -1683 kJ/mol**

Additional Problems

1. Calculate ΔH for the violent reaction of fluorine with water.

$$F_2(g) + H_2O(l) \rightarrow 2HF(g) + O_2(g)$$

2. Calculate ΔH for the reaction of calcium oxide and sulfur trioxide.

$$CaO(s) + SO_3(g) \rightarrow CaSO_4(s)$$

Use the following equations and data.

$$H_2O(l) + SO_3(g) \rightarrow H_2SO_4(l) \qquad\qquad \Delta H = -132.5 \text{ kJ/mol}$$
$$H_2SO_4(l) + Ca(s) \rightarrow CaSO_4(s) + H_2(g) \qquad \Delta H = -602.5 \text{ kJ/mol}$$
$$Ca(s) + O_2(g) \rightarrow CaO(s) \qquad\qquad\qquad \Delta H = -634.9 \text{ kJ/mol}$$
$$H_2(g) + O_2(g) \rightarrow H_2O(l) \qquad\qquad\qquad \Delta H = -285.8 \text{ kJ/mol}$$

3. Calculate ΔH for the reaction of sodium oxide with sulfur dioxide.

$$Na_2O(s) + SO_2(g) \rightarrow Na_2SO_3(s)$$

4. Use enthalpies of combustion to calculate ΔH for the oxidation of 1-butanol to make butanoic acid.

$$C_4H_9OH(l) + O_2(g) \rightarrow C_3H_7COOH(l) + H_2O(l)$$

Combustion of butanol:

$$C_4H_9OH(l) + 6O_2(g) \rightarrow 4CO_2(g) + 5H_2O(l)$$

$\Delta H_c = -2675.9 \text{ kJ/mol}$

Combustion of butanoic acid:

$$C_3H_7COOH(l) + 5O_2(g) \rightarrow 4CO_2(g) + 4H_2O(l)$$

$\Delta H_c = -2183.6 \text{ kJ/mol}$

5. Determine the free energy change for the reduction of CuO with hydrogen. Products and reactants are at 25°C.

$$CuO(s) + H_2(g) \rightarrow Cu(s) + H_2O(l)$$

$\Delta H = -128.5 \text{ kJ/mol}$
$\Delta S = -70.1 \text{ J/mol·K}$

6. Calculate the enthalpy change at 25°C for the reaction of sodium iodide and chlorine. Use only the data given.

$$NaI(s) + Cl_2(g) \rightarrow NaCl(s) + I_2(l)$$

$\Delta S = -79.9 \text{ J/mol·K}$
$\Delta G = -98.0 \text{ kJ/mol}$

7. The element bromine can be produced by the reaction of hydrogen bromide and manganese(IV) oxide.

$$4HBr(g) + MnO_2(s) \rightarrow MnBr_2(s) + 2H_2O(l) + Br_2(l)$$

ΔH for the reaction is -291.3 kJ/mol at 25°C. Use this value and values of ΔH_f^0 from **Table 1** to calculate ΔH_f^0 of $MnBr_2(s)$.

| Problem Solving *continued*

---

8. Calculate the change in entropy, ΔS, at 25°C for the reaction of calcium carbide with water to produce acetylene gas.

$$CaC_2(s) + 2H_2O(l) \rightarrow C_2H_2(g) + Ca(OH)_2(s)$$

$\Delta G = -147.7$ kJ/mol
$\Delta H = -125.6$ kJ/mol

9. Calculate the free energy change for the explosive decomposition of ammonium nitrate at 25°C. Note that H_2O is a gas in this reaction.

$$NH_4NO_3(s) \rightarrow N_2O(g) + 2H_2O(g)$$

$\Delta S = 446.4$ J/mol·K

10. In locations where natural gas, which is mostly methane, is not available, many people burn propane, which is delivered by truck and stored in a tank under pressure.

  a. Write the chemical equations for the complete combustion of 1 mol of methane, CH_4, and 1 mol of propane, C_3H_8.

  b. Calculate the enthalpy change for each reaction to determine the amount of heat evolved off by burning 1 mol of each fuel.

  c. Using the molar heats of combustion you calculated, determine the heat output per kilogram of each fuel. Which fuel yields more heat per unit mass?

11. The hydration of acetylene to form acetaldehyde is shown in the following equation:

$$C_2H_2(g) + H_2O(l) \rightarrow CH_3CHO(l)$$

Use heats of combustion for acetylene and acetaldehyde to compute the enthalpy of the above reaction.

$$C_2H_2(g) + 2O_2(g) \rightarrow 2CO_2(g) + H_2O(l)$$

$\Delta H_c = -1299.6$ kJ/mol

$$CH_3CHO(l) + 2O_2(g) \rightarrow 2CO_2(g) + 2H_2O(l)$$

$\Delta H_c = -1166.9$ kJ/mol

12. Calculate the enthalpy for the combustion of decane. ΔH_f^0 for liquid decane is -300.9 kJ/mol.

$$C_{10}H_{22}(l) + 15O_2(g) \rightarrow 10CO_2(g) + 11H_2O(l)$$

13. Find the enthalpy of the reaction of magnesium oxide with hydrogen chloride.

$$MgO(s) + 2HCl(g) \rightarrow MgCl_2(s) + H_2O(l)$$

Use the following equations and data.

$Mg(s) + 2HCl(g) \rightarrow MgCl_2(s) + H_2(g)$ $\qquad\qquad$ $\Delta H = -456.9$ kJ/mol
$Mg(s) + O_2(g) \rightarrow MgO(s)$ $\qquad\qquad$ $\Delta H = -601.6$ kJ/mol
$H_2O(l) \rightarrow H_2(g) + O_2(g)$ $\qquad\qquad$ $\Delta H = +285.8$ kJ/mol

---

| Problem Solving *continued*

14. What is the free energy change for the following reaction at 25°C?

$$2NaOH(s) + 2Na(s) \xrightarrow{\Delta} 2Na_2O(s) + H_2(g)$$

$\Delta S = 10.6$ J/mol·K

$\Delta H^0_{f_{NaOH}} = -425.9$ kJ/mol

15. The following equation represents the reaction between gaseous HCl and gaseous ammonia to form solid ammonium chloride.

$$NH_3(g) + HCl(g) \rightarrow NH_4Cl(s)$$

Calculate the entropy change in J/mol·K for the reaction of hydrogen chloride and ammonia at 25°C using the following data and the values fround in **Table 1.**

$\Delta G = -91.2$ kJ/mol

16. The production of steel from iron involves the removal of many impurities in the iron ore. The following equations show some of the purifying reactions. Calculate the enthalpy for each reaction. Use **Table 1** and the data given.

a. $3C(s) + Fe_2O_3(s) \rightarrow 3CO(g) + 2Fe(s)$

$\Delta H^0_{f_{CO(g)}} = -110.53$ kJ/mol

b. $3Mn(s) + Fe_2O_3(s) \rightarrow 3MnO(s) + 2Fe(s)$

$\Delta H^0_{f_{MnO(s)}} = -384.9$ kJ/mol

c. $12P(s) + 10Fe_2O_3(s) \rightarrow 3P_4O_{10}(s) + 20Fe(s)$

$\Delta H^0_{f_{P_4O_{10}(s)}} = -3009.9$ kJ/mol

d. $3Si(s) + 2Fe_2O_3(s) \rightarrow 3SiO_2(s) + 4Fe(s)$

$\Delta H^0_{f_{SiO_2(s)}} = -910.9$ kJ/mol

e. $3S(s) + 2Fe_2O_3(s) \rightarrow 3SO_2(g) + 4Fe(s)$

Quiz

Section: Energy Transfer

In the space provided, write the letter of the term or phrase that best answers the question.

_______ **1.** Energy is measured in units of
   a. joules.
   b. kelvins.
   c. pounds.
   d. All of the above

_______ **2.** The total energy of a sample is called its
   a. temperature.
   b. heat.
   c. enthalpy.
   d. joule.

_______ **3.** What symbol is used to represent enthalpy?
   a. K
   b. H
   c. E
   d. None of the above

_______ **4.** The temperature of a substance is
   a. dependent on its mass.
   b. an extensive property.
   c. an intensive property.
   d. equal to its heat.

_______ **5.** If two substances are at the same temperature, their enthalpy
   a. is the same.
   b. is different.
   c. cannot be measured.
   d. relationship cannot be determined from the information provided.

_______ **6.** The molar heat capacity of a substance is the energy as heat needed
   a. to raise the temperature of one gram by 1 K.
   b. to raise the temperature of one mole by 1 K.
   c. to raise the temperature of one gram by 1°F.
   d. to raise the temperature of one mole by 1°F.

▎Quiz *continued*

_______ **7.** How much energy as heat is needed to raise the temperature of one mole of argon from 25°C to 40°C? The molar heat capacity of argon is 20.8 J/K·mol.
   a. 20.8 J
   b. 208 J
   c. 312 J
   d. 416 J

_______ **8.** The specific heat capacity of a substance is the amount of heat needed
   a. to raise the temperature of one gram by 1 K.
   b. to raise the temperature of one mole by 1 K.
   c. to raise the temperature of one gram by 1°F.
   d. to raise the temperature of one mole by 1°F.

_______ **9.** If you know the specific heat capacity, you can calculate the molar heat capacity by
   a. dividing by the molar mass.
   b. multiplying by the molar mass.
   c. multiplying by 100.
   d. multiplying by the molar mass × 100.

_______ **10.** The molar heat capacity of iron (M = 55.8) is 25.1 J/K·mol. How much energy must be added to increase the temperature of 111.6 g of iron by 10 K?
   a. 10 J
   b. 251 J
   c. 502 J
   d. 1116 J

Quiz

Section: Using Enthalpy

In the space provided, write the letter of the term or phrase that best answers the question.

_______ **1.** For a given substance, the term ΔH refers to
  a. the total energy.
  b. the total enthalpy.
  c. the change in enthalpy.
  d. the change in temperature.

_______ **2.** Thermodynamics is the branch of science that
  a. examines the various process and the energy changes that accompany the process.
  b. examines heat only.
  c. examine only chemical processes and their energy changes.
  d. None of the above

_______ **3.** During heating, the change in enthalpy of a substance
  a. is proportional to the change in temperature.
  b. decreases as temperature increases.
  c. is independent of the change in temperature.
  d. increases faster than the change in temperature.

_______ **4.** How much energy does an aluminum (M = 27.0) sample gain if its molar heat capacity is 24.2 J/mol·K, its mass is 13.5 g, and it is heated from 10.0°C to 40.0°C?
  a. 24.2 J
  b. 242 J
  c. 363 J
  d. 726 J

_______ **5.** If a piece of aluminum is heated from 30.0°C to 50.0°C, what is the value of ΔT?
  a. 0.0 K
  b. 20.0 K
  c. 293.0 K
  d. 323.0 K

_______ **6.** The topics covered by the study of thermodynamics include
  a. energy changes during heating.
  b. energy changes during chemical reactions.
  c. color changes during chemical reactions.
  d. Both (a) and (b)

| Quiz *continued*

_______ **7.** If the enthalpy of one mole of a substance increases by 508 J when the substance is heated by 20 K, what is the molar heat capacity?
  a. 25.4 J/mol·K
  b. 254 J/mol·K
  c. 25.4 J/g·K
  d. 508 J/mol·K

_______ **8.** About what enthalpy increase would you expect when a solid block containing one mole of metal is heated by 400°C?
  a. 25 J
  b. 1000 J
  c. 10 000 J
  d. 25 000 J

_______ **9.** If the ΔH of a system is measured as -177 kJ, the change is
  a. endothermic.
  b. exothermic.
  c. either endothermic or exothermic.
  d. reversible.

_______ **10.** In the change in question 9, the total energy at the beginning is
  a. greater than the total energy at the end of the change.
  b. less than the total energy at the end of the change.
  c. equal to the total energy at the end of the change.
  d. None of the above

Quiz

Section: Changes in Enthalpy During Chemical Reactions

In the space provided, write the letter of the term or phrase that best answers the question.

_______ **1.** The energy absorbed or released during a reaction in which a substance is formed is called the
  a. calorie change.
  b. standard condition.
  c. enthalpy of formation.
  d. heat.

_______ **2.** During an endothermic reaction, total energy
  a. decreases.
  b. increases.
  c. stays the same.
  d. cannot be determined.

_______ **3.** The enthalpy of reaction for a chemical change can be determined by
  a. multiplying the total enthalpies of the products and reactants.
  b. subtracting the total enthalpy of the reactants from that of the products.
  c. subtracting the total enthalpy of the products from that of the reactants.
  d. adding the total enthalpies of the products and reactants.

_______ **4.** The total enthalpy of the products in a reaction is 388 kJ, and the total enthalpy of the reactants is 728 kJ. What is ΔH for the reaction?
  a. -1116 kJ
  b. $+340$ kJ
  c. -340 kJ
  d. $+1116$ kJ

_______ **5.** The enthalpy of formation of an element is
  a. negative.
  b. positive.
  c. zero.
  d. negative or positive, depending on which element.

Quiz *continued*

_______ **6.** The enthalpy of formation of a compound is -612 kJ/mol, and the products of its combustion have a total enthalpy of formation of -671 kJ. What is the enthalpy of combustion of this compound?
   a. -59 kJ/mol
   b. $+59$ kJ/ml
   c. -1283 kJ/mol
   d. $+1283$ kJ/mol

_______ **7.** Combustion reactions are
   a. always exothermic.
   b. always endothermic.
   c. sometimes exothermic and sometimes endothermic.
   d. adiabatic.

_______ **8.** Calorimeters can be used to determine the calorie content of food by using which type of reaction?
   a. digestion
   b. synthesis
   c. condensation
   d. combustion

_______ **9.** $\Delta H =$
   a. $H_{\text{reactants}} - H_{\text{products}}$
   b. $H_{\text{reactants}} + H_{\text{products}}$
   c. $H_{\text{products}} - H_{\text{reactants}}$
   d. $H_{\text{products}}/H_{\text{reactants}}$

_______ **10.** The standard thermodynamic temperature is
   a. 0 K.
   b. 25 K.
   c. 0°C.
   d. 25°C.

Quiz

Section: Order and Spontaneity

In the space provided, write the letter of the term or phrase that best answers the question.

_______ **1.** The term that describes disorder in a system is
   a. enthalpy.
   b. entropy.
   c. free energy.
   d. heat of reaction.

_______ **2.** Entropy increases as
   a. the temperature of the system increases.
   b. the temperature of the system decreases.
   c. the enthalpy of the system decreases.
   d. a chemical reaction proceeds.

_______ **3.** Entropy in a system increases when
   a. gases are diluted.
   b. ions disperse in a solution.
   c. the total moles of gaseous product exceed the total moles of
       gaseous reactant.
   d. All of the above

_______ **4.** According to Hess's Law, the entropy of a reaction
   a. can be calculated from the standard entropies of the products and
       the reactants.
   b. increases as thermal energy is removed.
   c. increases as temperature decreases.
   d. is equal to zero for elements.

_______ **5.** Compared with a single gas, a mixture of gases is
   a. more disordered.
   b. less disordered.
   c. equally disordered.
   d. less favorable.

Quiz *continued*

_______ **6.** A spontaneous reaction
  a. occurs immediately as the reactants are mixed.
  b. is likely to occur without continuous addition of energy.
  c. occurs only when the Gibbs energy is equal to zero.
  d. occurs only when the free energy is smaller than the enthalpy.

_______ **7.** A reaction cannot be spontaneous if ΔH is
  a. positive and ΔS is negative.
  b. negative and ΔS is negative.
  c. positive and ΔS is positive.
  d. negative and ΔS is positive.

_______ **8.** If the Gibbs energy of a reaction is positive, the reaction
  a. is nonspontaneous.
  b. occurs spontaneously.
  c. is at equilibrium.
  d. is reversible.

_______ **9.** What is the value of ΔG at 250 K for a reaction in which $\Delta H = +185$ kJ/mol and $\Delta S = +2.00$ kJ/mol·K?
  a. +315 kJ/mol
  b. −315 kJ/mol
  c. −685 kJ/mol
  d. +685 kJ/mol

_______ **10.** What is the value of ΔG at 250 K for a reaction in which $\Delta H = -185$ kJ/mol and $\Delta S = +2.00$ kJ/mol·K?
  a. +315 kJ/mol
  b. −315 kJ/mol
  c. −685 kJ/mol
  d. −685 kJ

Chapter Test

Causes of Change

In the space provided, write the letter of the term or phrase that best completes each statement or best answers each question.

______ **1.** A chemical change is likely to occur when
  a. energy and disorder both increase.
  b. energy and disorder both decrease.
  c. energy increases and disorder decreases.
  d. energy decreases and disorder increases.

______ **2.** If object A has a higher temperature than object B, then object A
  a. contains more energy as heat than object B.
  b. contains less energy as heat than object B.
  c. contains the same amount of energy as heat as object B.
  d. may contain more, less, or the same amount of energy as heat as object B.

______ **3.** An example of increasing entropy is the
  a. formation of crystals from a solution.
  b. formation of 1 mol of gas from 1 mol of one reactant gas and 1 mol of another reactant gas.
  c. diffusion of crystals in a solution.
  d. None of the above

______ **4.** The total energy of a substance is its
  a. enthalpy.
  b. free energy.
  c. temperature.
  d. All of the above

______ **5.** To determine the amount of energy as heat associated with the change taking place in a calorimeter, the information that is *not* needed is the
  a. specific heat of calorimeter.
  b. volume of the water in the calorimeter.
  c. specific heat of water.
  d. change in temperature of the water.

______ **6.** How much energy as heat is needed to raise the temperature of one mole of argon from 25°C to 40°C? The molar heat capacity of argon is 20.8 J/K·mol.
  a. 20.8 J
  b. 208 J
  c. 312 J
  d. 416 J

Chapter Test *continued*

_______ **7.** An increase in temperature in a system causes a(n)
 a. increase in both entropy and enthalpy.
 b. decrease in both entropy and enthalpy.
 c. increase in entropy and a decrease in enthalpy.
 d. decrease in entropy and an increase in enthalpy.

_______ **8.** The change in Gibbs energy for a substance can be found by the expression
 a. $\Delta H - T\Delta S$.
 b. $\Delta H + T\Delta S$.
 c. $\Delta S - T\Delta H$.
 d. $\Delta S + T\Delta H$.

_______ **9.** A chemical reaction occurs spontaneously when ΔG is
 a. positive.
 b. negative.
 c. zero.
 d. constant.

_______ **10.** A chemical reaction is exothermic when ΔH is
 a. positive.
 b. negative.
 c. zero.
 d. constant.

_______ **11.** The term *thermodynamics* refers to the study of
 a. energy changes.
 b. only physical changes.
 c. only chemical changes.
 d. None of the above

_______ **12.** When an iceberg composed of pure water ($C = 18.1$ kJ/K·mol) is heated from $-25°C$ to $-15°C$, the molar enthalpy change is
 a. 18.1 kJ.
 b. 181 kJ.
 c. 271 kJ.
 d. impossible to calculate without the mass of the iceberg.

_______ **13.** The standard enthalpy of formation of Cl_2 is
 a. positive.
 b. negative.
 c. zero.
 d. undetermined without more information.

❙ Chapter Test *continued*

Use the data in Table 1 to answer questions 14–17.

TABLE 1 STANDARD ENTHALPIES AND ENTROPIES

Substance	Standard enthalpy of formation (kJ/mol)	Standard entropy (J/mol)
$H_2(g)$	0	130.7
$O_2(g)$	0	205.1
$H_2O(g)$	-242	188.7
$CO_2(g)$	-393	213.8
$C(s)$ (graphite)	0	5.7

_______**14.** For the reaction, $H_2(g) + \frac{1}{2}O_2(g) \rightarrow H_2O(g)$, the values of ΔH and ΔS are
  a. 242 kJ and 148.3 J.
  b. 242 kJ and -148.3 J.
  c. -242 kJ and 46.4 J.
  d. -242 kJ and -44.5 J.

_______**15.** The reaction, $C(s) + O_2(g) \rightarrow CO_2(g)$ is
  a. spontaneous.
  b. not spontaneous.
  c. is spontaneous at 298 K, but not at 25°C.
  d. There is insufficient information to determine whether the reaction is spontaneous.

_______**16.** For the reaction $H_2O(g) \rightarrow H_2(g) + \frac{1}{2}O_2(g)$ the value of ΔG is
  a. positive.
  b. negative.
  c. positive at low temperatures and negative at high temperatures.
  d. negative at low temperatures and positive at high temperatures.

_______**17.** The reaction, $CO_2(g) \rightarrow C(s) + O_2(g)$ is
  a. exothermic.
  b. endothermic.
  c. isothermic.
  d. spontaneous.

_______**18.** For a exothermic reaction,
  a. ΔG is always positive.
  b. ΔH is always negative.
  c. ΔS is always positive.
  d. All of the above

❙ Chapter Test *continued*

_______**19.** All of the following factors must be known to determine molar heat capacity, except
    a. mass.
    b. amount of energy as heat needed to raise the temperature.
    c. volume.
    d. temperature change.

_______**20.** If a chemical reaction is spontaneous, it
    a. occurs as soon as the reactants come together.
    b. occurs without the continuous addition of energy.
    c. involves an increase in entropy.
    d. is endothermic.

| Chapter Test *continued*

Answer the questions in the spaces provided.

21. How does temperature differ from heat?

____

____

22. Why is it necessary to know the temperature of the reactants and the products of a reaction in order to determine change in the Gibbs energy of the reaction.

____

____

Answer each of the following problems in the spaces provided.

23. For a reaction that has a ΔH of 23 kJ and a ΔS of -130 J/K, calculate ΔG at 25°C.

24. The molar heat capacity for silver (M = 107.9) is 25.3 J/K·mol. Calculate the amount of energy as heat that is needed to raise the temperature of 175 g of silver from 22.5°C to 40.0°C.

25. When burned in a calorimeter, a walnut raises the temperature of 2500 g of water from 25.0°C to 74.0°C. How much energy is released by the walnut? The molar heat capacity of water is 75.3 J/K·mol.

Skills Practice Lab

Calorimetry and Hess's Law

A man working for a cleaning firm was told by his employer to pour some old cleaning supplies into a glass container for disposal. Some of the supplies included muriatic (hydrochloric) acid, $HCl(aq)$, and a drain cleaner containing lye, $NaOH(s)$. When the substances were mixed, the container shattered, spilling the contents onto the worker's arms and legs. The worker claims that the hot spill caused burns, and he is, therefore, suing his employer. The employer claims that the worker is lying because the solutions were at room temperature before they were mixed. The employer says that a chemical burn is unlikely because tests after the accident revealed that the mixture had a neutral pH, indicating that the HCl and NaOH were neutralized. The court has asked you to evaluate whether the worker's story is supported by scientific evidence.

Chemicals can be dangerous because of their special storage needs. Acids cannot be stored in metal containers, and organic solvents cannot be kept in plastic containers. Chemicals that are mixed and react are even more dangerous because many reactions release large amounts of heat. Glass, although relatively nonreactive with solutions of pure substances, is heat-sensitive and can shatter if there is a sudden change in temperature due to a reaction. Some glassware, such as Pyrex, is heat-conditioned but can still fracture under extreme heat conditions, especially if scratched.

You will measure the amount of heat released by mixing the chemicals in two ways. First you will break the reaction into steps and measure the heat change of each step. Then you will measure the heat change of the reaction when it takes place all at once. When you are finished, you will be able to use the calorimetry equation from the chapter "Causes of Change" to determine the following:

- the amount of heat evolved during the overall reaction

- the amount of heat for each step

- the amount of heat for the reaction in kilojoules per mole

- whether this heat could have raised the temperature of the water in the solution high enough to cause a burn

OBJECTIVES

Demonstrate proficiency in the use of calorimeters and related equipment.

Relate temperature changes to enthalpy changes.

Determine the heat of reaction for several reactions.

Demonstrate that the heat of reaction can be additive.

Always wear safety goggles and lab apron to protect your eyes and clothing. If you get a chemical in your eyes, immediately flush the chemical out at the eyewash station while calling to your teacher. Know the location of the emergency lab shower and eyewash station and the procedures for using them.

Calorimetry and Hess's Law *continued*

Do not touch any chemicals. If you get a chemical on your skin or clothing, wash the chemical off at the sink while calling to your teacher. Make sure you carefully read the labels and follow the precautions on all containers of chemicals that you use. If there are no precautions stated on the label, ask your teacher what precautions to follow. Do not taste any chemicals or items used in the laboratory. Never return leftovers to their original container; take only small amounts to avoid wasting supplies.

Call your teacher in the event of a spill. Spills should be cleaned up promptly, according to your teacher's directions.

Acids and bases are corrosive. If an acid or base spills onto your skin or clothing, wash the area immediately with running water. Call your teacher in the event of an acid spill. Acid or base spills should be cleaned up promptly.

Do not heat glassware that is broken, chipped, or cracked. Use tongs or a hot mitt to handle heated glassware and other equipment because hot glassware does not always look hot.

When using a Bunsen burner, confine long hair and loose clothing. If your clothing catches fire, WALK to the emergency lab shower and use it to put out the fire.

MATERIALS

- balance
- distilled water
- glass stirring rod
- graduated cylinder, 100 mL
- HCl solution, 0.50 M
- HCl solution, 1.0 M
- NaOH pellets
- NaOH solution, 1.0 M
- plastic-foam cups (or calorimeters)
- spatula
- thermometer
- watch glass

Optional Equipment

- CBL unit
- graphing calculator with link cable
- Vernier temperature probe

| Calorimetry and Hess's Law *continued*

Procedure

ADVANCE PREPARATION

1. Put on safety goggles, gloves, and lab apron.

2. If you are not using a plastic-foam cup as a calorimeter, ask your teacher for instructions on using the calorimeter. At various points in the procedure, you will need to measure the temperature of the solution within the calorimeter.

Thermometer Procedure continues on page 39.

CBL AND SENSORS PROCEDURE

3. Connect the CBL to the graphing calculator with the unit-to-unit link cable using the I/O ports located on each unit. Connect the temperature probe to the CH1 port. Turn on the CBL and the graphing calculator. Start the program CHEMBIO on the graphing calculator.

    a. Select option *SET UP PROBES* from the MAIN MENU. Enter 1 for the number of probes. Select the temperature probe from the list. Enter 1 for the channel number. Select *USE STORED* from the CALIBRATION menu.

    b. Select the *COLLECT DATA* option from the MAIN MENU. Select the *TRIGGER* option from the DATA COLLECTION menu.

4. Measure the temperature by gently inserting the Vernier temperature probe into the hole in the calorimeter lid.

Reaction 1: Dissolving NaOH

5. Pour about 100 mL of distilled water into a graduated cylinder. Measure and record the volume of the water to the nearest 0.1 mL. Pour the water into your calorimeter.

6. Using the temperature probe, measure the temperature of the water. Press TRIGGER on the CBL to collect the temperature reading. Record this temperature in your data table. Select *STOP* from the TRIGGER menu on the graphing calculator. Leave the probe in the calorimeter.

7. Select the *COLLECT DATA* option from the MAIN MENU. Select the *TIME GRAPH* option from the DATA COLLECTION menu. Enter 6 for the time between samples, in seconds. Enter 99 for the number of samples (the CBL will collect data for 9.9 min). Press ENTER. Select *USE TIME SETUP* to continue. If you want to change the number of samples or the time between samples, select *MODIFY SETUP.* Enter 0 for *Ymin*, enter 100 for *Ymax*, and enter 5 for *Yscl.*

8. Determine and record the mass of a clean and dry watch glass to the nearest 0.01 g. Remove the watch glass from the balance. While wearing gloves, obtain about 2 g of NaOH pellets, and put them on the watch glass.

Calorimetry and Hess's Law *continued*

Use forceps when handling NaOH pellets. Measure and record the mass of the watch glass and the pellets to the nearest 0.01 g. **It is important that this step be done quickly because NaOH is hygroscopic. It absorbs moisture from the air, and its mass increases as long as it remains exposed to the air.**

9. Press ENTER on the graphing calculator to begin collecting the temperature readings for the water in the calorimeter.

10. Immediately place the NaOH pellets in the calorimeter cup, and gently stir the solution with a stirring rod. Place the lid on the calorimeter.

11. When the CBL displays DONE, use the arrow keys to trace the graph. Time in seconds in graphed on the x-axis, and the temperature readings are graphed on the y-axis. Record the highest temperature reading from the CBL in your data table.

12. When the reaction is finished, pour the solution into the container designated by your teacher for disposal of basic solutions.

13. Be sure to clean all equipment and rinse it with distilled water before continuing with the next procedure.

Reaction 2: NaOH and HCl in solution

14. Pour about 50 mL of 1.0 M HCl into a graduated cylinder. Measure and record the volume of the HCl solution to the nearest 0.1 mL. Pour the HCl solution into your calorimeter.

15. Select the *COLLECT DATA* option from the MAIN MENU. Select the *TRIGGER* option from the DATA COLLECTION menu. Using the temperature probe, measure the temperature of the HCl solution. Press TRIGGER on the CBL to collect the temperature reading. Record this temperature in your data table.

16. Pour about 50 mL of 1.0 M NaOH into a graduated cylinder. Measure and record the volume of the NaOH solution to the nearest 0.1 mL. **For this step only, rinse the temperature probe in distilled water.** Using the temperature probe, measure the temperature of the NaOH solution. Press TRIGGER on the CBL to collect the temperature reading. Record this temperature in your data table. Select *STOP* from the TRIGGER menu on the graphing calculator. Put the probe in the calorimeter.

17. Select the *COLLECT DATA* option from the MAIN MENU. Select the *TIME GRAPH* option from the DATA COLLECTION menu. Enter 6 for the time between samples, in seconds. Enter 99 for the number of samples. Press ENTER. Select *USE TIME SETUP* to continue. If you want to change the number of samples or the time between samples, select *MODIFY SETUP.* Enter 0 for *Ymin*, enter 100 for *Ymax*, and enter 5 for *Yscl.* Press ENTER on the calculator to begin collecting temperature readings.

18. Pour the NaOH solution into the calorimeter cup, and stir gently. Place the lid on the calorimeter.

19. When the CBL displays DONE, use the arrow keys to trace the graph. Time in seconds in graphed on the x-axis, and the temperature readings are graphed on the y-axis. Record the highest temperature reading from the CBL in your data table.

20. Pour the solution into the container designated by your teacher for disposal of mostly neutral solutions. Clean and rinse all equipment before continuing with the next procedure.

Reaction 3: Solid NaOH and HCl in solution

21. Pour about 100 mL of 0.50 M HCl into a graduated cylinder. Measure and record the volume to the nearest 0.1 mL. Pour the HCl solution into your calorimeter.

22. Select the *COLLECT DATA* option from the MAIN MENU. Select the *TRIGGER* option from the DATA COLLECTION menu. Using the temperature probe, measure the temperature of the HCl solution. Press TRIGGER on the CBL to collect the temperature reading. Record this temperature in your data table. Select *STOP* from the TRIGGER menu on the graphing calculator.

23. Select the *COLLECT DATA* option from the MAIN MENU. Select the *TIME GRAPH* option from the DATA COLLECTION menu. Enter 6 for the time between samples, in seconds. Enter 99 for the number of samples. Press ENTER. Select *USE TIME SETUP* to continue. If you want to change the number of samples or the time between samples, select *MODIFY SETUP.* Enter 0 for *Ymin*, enter 100 for *Ymax*, and enter 5 for *Yscl.* Press ENTER on the calculator to begin collecting temperature readings.

24. Measure the mass of a clean and dry watch glass, and record it in your data table. Obtain approximately 2 g of NaOH. Place it on the watch glass, and record the total mass to the nearest 0.01 g. **It is important that this step be done quickly because NaOH is hygroscopic.**

25. Press ENTER on the graphing calculator to begin collecting the temperature readings for the water in the calorimeter.

26. Immediately place the NaOH pellets in the calorimeter, and gently stir the solution. Place the lid on the calorimeter.

27. When the CBL displays DONE, use the arrow keys to trace the graph. Time in seconds in graphed on the x-axis, and the temperature readings are graphed on the y-axis. Record the highest temperature reading from the CBL in your data table.

28. When the reaction is finished, pour the solution into the container designated by your teacher for disposal of basic solutions.

29. Clean all apparatus and your lab station. Check with your teacher for the proper disposal procedures. Any excess NaOH pellets should be disposed of in the designated container. Always wash your hands thoroughly after cleaning up the lab area and equipment.

| Calorimetry and Hess's Law *continued*

THERMOMETER PROCEDURE

3. Measure the temperature by gently inserting the thermometer into the hole in
the calorimeter lid. The thermometer takes time to reach the same temperature as the solution inside the calorimeter, so wait to be sure you have an
accurate reading. **Thermometers break easily, so be careful with them,
and do not use them to stir a solution.**

Reaction 1: Dissolving NaOH

4. Pour about 100 mL of distilled water into a graduated cylinder. Measure and
record the volume of the water to the nearest 0.1 mL. Pour the water into your
calorimeter. Measure and record the water temperature to the nearest 0.1°C.

5. Determine and record the mass of a clean and dry watch glass to the nearest
0.01 g. Remove the watch glass from the balance. While wearing gloves,
obtain about 2 g of NaOH pellets, and put them on the watch glass. Use
forceps when handling NaOH pellets. Measure and record the mass of the
watch glass and the pellets to the nearest 0.01 g. **It is important that this
step be done quickly because NaOH is hygroscopic. It absorbs moisture from the air, and increases its mass as long as it remains exposed
to the air.**

6. Immediately place the NaOH pellets in the calorimeter cup, and gently stir the
solution with a stirring rod. **Do not stir with a thermometer.** Place the lid
on the calorimeter. Watch the thermometer, and record the highest temperature in the data table. When the reaction is finished, pour the solution into the
container designated by your teacher for disposal of basic solutions.

7. Be sure to clean all equipment and rinse it with distilled water before continuing with the next procedure.

Reaction 2: NaOH and HCl in solution

8. Pour about 50 mL of 1.0 M HCl into a graduated cylinder. Measure and record
the volume of the HCl solution to the nearest 0.1 mL. Pour the HCl solution
into your calorimeter. Measure and record the temperature of the HCl solution to the nearest 0.1°C.

9. Pour about 50 mL of 1.0 M NaOH into a graduated cylinder. Measure and
record the volume of the NaOH solution to the nearest 0.1 mL. **For this step
only, rinse the thermometer in distilled water, and measure the temperature of the NaOH solution in the graduated cylinder to the nearest 0.1°C. Record the temperature in your data table, and then replace
the thermometer in the calorimeter.**

10. Pour the NaOH solution into the calorimeter cup, and stir gently. Place the lid
on the calorimeter. Watch the thermometer, and record the highest temperature
in the data table. When finished with this reaction, pour the solution into the
container designated by your teacher for disposal of mostly neutral solutions.

11. Clean and rinse all equipment before continuing with the next procedure.

Calorimetry and Hess's Law *continued*

Reaction 3: Solid NaOH and HCl in solution

12. Pour about 100 mL of 0.50 M HCl into a graduated cylinder. Measure and record the volume to the nearest 0.1 mL. Pour the HCl solution into your calorimeter, as shown in Figure B. Measure and record the temperature of the HCl solution to the nearest 0.1°C.

13. Measure the mass of a clean and dry watch glass, and record it in your data table. Obtain approximately 2 g of NaOH. Place it on the watch glass, and record the total mass to the nearest 0.01 g. **It is important that this step be done quickly because NaOH is hygroscopic.**

14. Immediately place the NaOH pellets in the calorimeter, and gently stir the solution. Place the lid on the calorimeter. Watch the thermometer, and record the highest temperature in the data table. When finished with this reaction, pour the solution into the container designated by your teacher for disposal of mostly neutral solutions.

15. Clean all apparatus and your lab station. Check with your teacher for the proper disposal procedures. Any excess NaOH pellets should be disposed of in the designated container. Always wash your hands thoroughly after cleaning up the lab area and equipment.

TABLE 1 TEMPERATURE DATA FOR EACH REACTION

	Reaction 1	Reaction 2	Reaction 3
Mass of empty watch glass			
Mass of watch glass with NaOH			
Total volumes of liquid(s)			
Initial temperature			
Final temperature			

Analysis

1. Organizing Data Write a balanced chemical equation for each of the three reactions that you performed. (Hint: Be sure to include states of matter for all substances in each equation.)

Calorimetry and Hess's Law *continued*

2. **Analyzing Results** Find a way to get the equation for the total reaction by adding two of the equations from Analysis item 1 and then canceling out substances that appear in the same form on both sides of the new equation. (Hint: Start with the equation whose product is a reactant in a second equation. Add those two equations together.)

3. **Explaining Events** Explain why a plastic-foam cup makes a better calorimeter than a paper cup does.

____

____

____

4. **Organizing Data** Calculate the change in temperature (Δt) for each of the reactions.

5. **Organizing Data** Assuming that the density of the water and the solutions is 1.00 g/mL, calculate the mass, m, of liquid present for each of the reactions.

6. **Analyzing Results** Using the calorimeter equation (Heat $= m \times \Delta t \times c_{p,\mathrm{H_2O}}$), calculate the heat released by each reaction. (Hint: Use the specific heat capacity of water in your calculations; $c_{p,\mathrm{H_2O}} = 4.180$ J/g·°C.)

| Calorimetry and Hess's Law *continued*

7. Organizing Data Calculate the moles of NaOH used in each of the reactions. (Hint: To find the number of moles in a solution, multiply the volume in liters by the molar concentration.)

8. Analyzing Results Calculate the ΔH value in terms of kilojoules per mole of NaOH for each of the three reactions.

9. Analyzing Results Using your answer to Analysis item 2 and your knowledge of Hess's law from the chapter "Causes of Change," explain how the enthalpies for the three reactions should be mathematically related.

____

____

10. Analyzing Results Which of the following types of heat of reaction apply to the enthalpies calculated in Analysis item 8: heat of combustion, heat of solution, heat of reaction, heat of fusion, heat of vaporization, and heat of formation?

____

____

Conclusions

11. Evaluating Methods Use your answers from Analysis items 7 and 8 to determine the ΔH value for the reaction of solid NaOH with HCl solution by direct measurement and by indirect calculation.

Calorimetry and Hess's Law *continued*

12. Drawing Conclusions Third-degree burns can occur if skin comes into contact for more than 4 s with water that is hotter than 60°C (140°F). Suppose someone accidentally poured hydrochloric acid into a glass-disposal container that already contained the drain cleaner NaOH and the container shattered. The solution in the container was approximately 55 g of NaOH and 450 mL of hydrochloric acid solution containing 1.35 mol of HCl (a 3.0 M HCl solution). If the initial temperature of the solutions was 25°C, could a mixture hot enough to cause burns have resulted?

13. Applying Conclusions For the reaction between the drain cleaner and HCl described in item 12, which chemical is the limiting reactant? How many moles of the other reactant remained unreacted?

____

____

14. Evaluating Results When chemists make solutions from NaOH pellets, they often keep the solution in an ice bath. Explain why.

____

____

15. Evaluating Methods You have worked with heats of solution for exothermic reactions. Could the same type of procedure be used to determine the temperature changes for endothermic reactions? How would the procedure stay the same? What would change about the procedure and the data?

____

____

____

| Calorimetry and Hess's Law *continued*

---

16. Drawing Conclusions Which is more stable, solid NaOH or NaOH solution? Explain your answer.

____

____

Extensions

1. Applying Conclusions When a strongly acidic or basic solution is spilled on a person, the first step is to dilute it by washing the area of the spill with a lot of water. Explain why adding an acid or a base to neutralize the solution immediately is not a good idea.

____

____

____

2. Designing Experiments A chemical supply company is going to ship NaOH pellets to a very humid place, and you have been asked to give advice on packaging. Design a package for the NaOH pellets. Explain the advantages of your package's design and materials. (Hint: Remember that the reaction in which NaOH absorbs moisture from the air is exothermic and that NaOH reacts exothermically with other compounds as well.)

____

____

____

____

____

Skills Practice Lab

Energy Content of Foods

You are a lab technician working for NASA. Recently you were given the job of deciding what type of foods should be included in the next space mission. Four food types have been selected as possible snacks for the astronauts. You need to determine which of these four food choices has the highest energy content while adding the least amount of mass to the mission.

Your team will test two of the food types using a method known as calorimetry. During this process, you will burn a food sample positioned below a can containing a given amount of cold water. The water temperature will be monitored during the experiment using a temperature probe. By calculating the temperature change of the water, you will determine how much energy was released when the food sample burned.

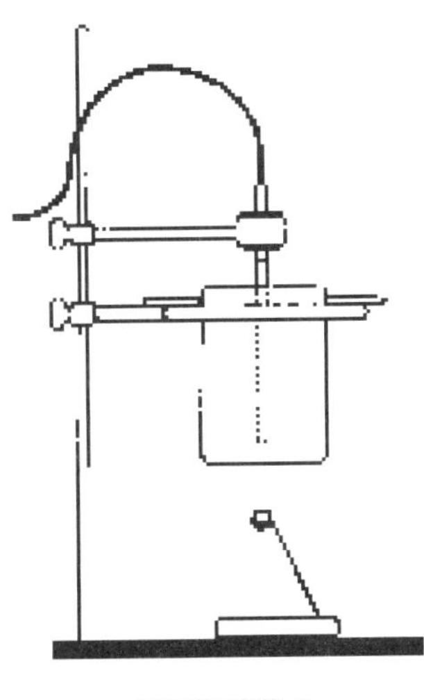

FIGURE 1

OBJECTIVES

- **Measure** temperature changes.
- **Calculate** energy changes using specific heat.
- **Infer** the energy content of food.
- **Relate** energy content to types of food.
- **Evaluate** whether the nutrition labels are accurate.

MATERIALS

- can, small
- food samples (2)
- matches
- water, cold
- wooden splint

Energy Content of Foods *continued*

EQUIPMENT

- food holder (see **Figure 1**)
- graduated cylinder, 100 mL
- LabPro or CBL2 interface
- stirring rods (2)
- ring stand and 4-inch ring
- TI graphing calculator
- utility clamp and slit stopper
- Vernier temperature probe

SAFETY

- Wear safety goggles when working around chemicals, acids, bases, flames, or heating devices. Contents under pressure may become projectiles and cause serious injury.

- Secure loose clothing, and remove dangling jewelry. Do not wear open-toed shoes or sandals in the lab.

- Wear an apron or lab coat to protect your clothing when working with chemicals.

- In order to avoid burns, wear heat-resistant gloves whenever instructed to do so.

- If you are unsure of whether an object is hot, do not touch it.

- Avoid wearing hair spray or hair gel on lab days.

- Whenever possible, use an electric hot plate as a heat source instead of an open flame.

- Never return unused chemicals to the original container; follow instructions for proper disposal.

Procedure

EQUIPMENT PREPARATION

1. Obtain and wear goggles.

2. Plug the temperature probe into Channel 1 of the LabPro or CBL 2 interface. Use the link cable to connect the TI graphing calculator to the interface. Firmly press in the cable ends.

3. Turn on the calculator, and start the DATAMATE program. Press $\boxed{\text{CLEAR}}$ to reset the program.

4. Set up the calculator and interface for the temperature probe.

    a. Select SETUP from the main screen.

    b. If the calculator displays a temperature probe in CH 1, proceed directly to Step 5. If it does not, continue with this step to set up your sensor manually.

    c. Press $\boxed{\text{ENTER}}$ to select CH 1.

    d. Select TEMPERATURE from the SELECT SENSOR menu.

    e. Select the temperature probe you are using (in °C) from the TEMPERATURE menu.

Energy Content of Foods *continued*

5. Set up the data-collection mode.

   a. To select MODE, press ⬆ once and press ENTER.

   b. Select TIME GRAPH from the SELECT MODE menu.

   c. Select CHANGE TIME SETTINGS from the TIME GRAPH SETTINGS menu.

   d. Enter "6" as the time between samples in seconds.

   e. Enter "100" as the number of samples. The length of the data collection will be 10 minutes.

   f. Select OK to return to the setup screen.

   g. Select OK again to return to the main screen.

6. Obtain a piece of one of the two foods assigned to you and a food holder like the one shown in **Figure 1**. Find and record the initial mass of the food sample and food holder. **CAUTION:** *Do not eat or drink in the laboratory.*

7. Determine and record the mass of an empty can. Obtain cold water from your teacher, and add 50 mL of it to the can. Determine and record the mass of the can and water.

8. Set up the apparatus as shown in **Figure 1**. Use a ring and stirring rod to suspend the can about 2.5 cm (1 in.) above the food sample. Use a utility clamp to suspend the temperature probe in the water. The probe should not touch the bottom of the can. Remember that the temperature probe must be in the water for at least 30 seconds before you complete Step 9.

DATA TABLE 1

Food sample 1:			
Initial mass of food sample and holder:			
Mass of empty can:		Mass of can and water:	
Food sample 2:			
Initial mass of food sample and holder:			
Mass of empty can:		Mass of can and water:	

DATA COLLECTION

9. Select START to begin collecting data. Record the initial temperature of the water, T_1, in Data Table 2 (round to the nearest 0.1°C). **Note:** You can monitor temperature in the upper-right corner of the real-time graph displayed on the calculator screen. Remove the food sample from under the can, and use a wooden splint to light it. Quickly place the burning food sample directly under the center of the can. Allow the water to be heated until the food sample stops burning.

10. Continue stirring the water until the temperature stops rising. Record this maximum temperature, T_2. Data collection will stop after 10 minutes (or press the STOP key to stop *before* 10 minutes have elapsed).

11. Determine and record the final mass of the food sample and food holder.

12. To confirm the initial (T_1) and final (T_2) values you recorded earlier, examine the data points along the curve on the displayed graph. As you move the cursor right or left, the time (X) and temperature (Y) values of each data point are displayed below the graph.

13. Press ENTER to return to the main screen. Select START to repeat the data collection for the second food sample. Use a new 50 mL portion of cold water. Repeat Steps 6–12.

14. When you are done, place burned food, used matches, and partially burned wooden splints in the container provided by the teacher.

DATA TABLE 2

Food sample 1:			
T_1:	T_2:	Final mass of sample and holder:	
Food sample 2:			
T_1:	T_2:	Final mass of sample and holder:	

Analysis

1. Organizing data Find the mass of water heated for each sample. __________

____

2. Organizing data Find the change in temperature of the water, ΔT, for each

sample. ____

____

3. Organizing data Find the mass (in g) of each food sample burned. __________

____

4. Analyzing Results Calculate the heat absorbed by the water, q, using the equation

$$q = C_p m \Delta T$$

where q is heat, C_p is the specific heat, m is the mass of water, and ΔT is the change in temperature. For water, C_p is 4.18 J/g°C. Convert your final answer

to units of kJ. ____

____

____

Energy Content of Foods *continued*

5. Analyzing Results Use the results of the previous two steps to calculate the

energy content (in kJ/g) of each food sample. _________________________________

____

DATA TABLE 3

Food sample 1:					
Mass of water heated:		g	Temperature change, ΔT:		°C
Mass of food burned:		g	Heat, q:		kJ
Energy content of food sample:					kJ/g
Food sample 2:					
Mass of water heated:		g	Temperature change, ΔT:		°C
Mass of food burned:		g	Heat, q:		kJ
Energy content of food sample:					kJ/g

Conclusions

1. Evaluating results Record your results and the results of other groups in the Class Results Table below. Which food had the highest energy content? Which

had the lowest energy content? ____

____

CLASS RESULTS TABLE

Marshmallows	Peanuts	Cashews	Popcorn
kJ/g	kJ/g	kJ/g	kJ/g
kJ/g	kJ/g	kJ/g	kJ/g
kJ/g	kJ/g	kJ/g	kJ/g
kJ/g	kJ/g	kJ/g	kJ/g
kJ/g	kJ/g	kJ/g	kJ/g

Average for each food type:

kJ/g	kJ/g	kJ/g	kJ/g

2. Evaluating results Food energy is often expressed in a unit called a Calorie (or dietary calorie). There are 4.18 kJ in one Calorie. Based on the class average for popcorn, calculate the number of Calories in a 50.0 g package

of popcorn. ____

____

Energy Content of Foods *continued*

3. Evaluating results Two of the foods in the experiment have a high fat content (peanuts and cashews), and two have a high carbohydrate content (marshmallows and popcorn). From your results, what generalization can you make

about the relative energy content of fats and carbohydrates? _____________

____

____

4. Evaluating results Based on the data you and your classmates collected, which of the four foods tested would you suggest to send on the NASA space mission?

____

____

Extensions

1. Applying results If you were packing for a mountain hike, what kind of

snacks would you bring along? Why? ___________________________

____

____

2. Critiquing methods Was all of the heat given off by the burning food sample transferred to the water in the can? How could this experiment be improved to account for all the heat given off when the food sample was burned?

____

____

____

____

3. Applying results Listed on the following page are possible nutrition labels for each of the food samples that you tested. Based on the data you and your classmates obtained in this lab, determine which of these labels is accurate and which is not. If you find a label to be incorrect, explain your reasoning.

____

____

____

Energy Content of Foods *continued*

MARSHMALLOWS

Nutrition Facts	
Serving Size 1 ounce	
Servings Per Container 6	
Amount per serving	
Calories 260	Calories from Fat 160
	% Daily Value
Total Fat 18g	13%
Saturated Fat 5g	27%
Cholesterol 0mg	0%
Sodium 260mg	11%
Total Carbohydrate 23g	8%
Dietary Fiber 1g	11%
Sugars 18g	
Protein 1g	

PEANUTS

Nutrition Facts	
Serving Size 1 ounce	
Servings Per Container 16	
Amount per serving	
Calories 165	Calories from Fat 125
	% Daily Value
Total Fat 14g	20%
Saturated Fat 1.9g	10%
Cholesterol 0mg	0%
Sodium 122mg	5%
Total Carbohydrate 5g	2%
Dietary Fiber 1g	4%
Sugars 2g	
Protein 8g	

CASHEWS

Nutrition Facts	
Serving Size 1 ounce	
Servings Per Container 16	
Amount per serving	
Calories 80	Calories from Fat 26
	% Daily Value
Total Fat 3g	4%
Saturated Fat 0.5g	3%
Cholesterol 0mg	0%
Sodium 177mg	7%
Total Carbohydrate 8g	3%
Dietary Fiber 2g	8%
Sugars 2g	
Protein 5g	

POPCORN

Nutrition Facts	
Serving Size 1 cup	
Servings Per Container 8	
Amount per serving	
Calories 30	Calories from Fat 0
	% Daily Value
Total Fat 0.3g	*%
Saturated Fat 0g	*%
Cholesterol 0mg	0%
Sodium 0mg	*%
Total Carbohydrate 6g	2%
Dietary Fiber 1g	4%
Sugars 2g	
Protein 0g	
***Less than 1% of US RDA**	

Lesson Plan

Section: Energy Transfer

Pacing

Regular Schedule	**with lab(s): NA**	**without lab(s):** 1 day
Block Schedule	**with lab(s): NA**	**without lab(s):** ½ day

Objectives

1. Define *enthalpy.*

2. Distinguish between heat and temperature.

3. Perform calculations using molar heat capacity.

National Science Education Standards Covered
UNIFYING CONCEPTS AND PROCESSES

UCP 1 Systems, order, and organization

UCP 2 Evidence, models, and explanation

UCP 3 Change, constancy, and measurement

PHYSICAL SCIENCE—CONSERVATION OF ENERGY AND THE INCREASE IN DISORDER

PS 5b All energy can be considered to be either kinetic energy, which is the energy of motion; potential energy, which depends on relative position; or energy contained by a field, such as electromagnetic waves.

PS 5c Heat consists of random motion and the vibrations of atoms, molecules, and ions. The higher the temperature, the greater the atomic or molecular motion.

KEY
SE = Student Edition
ATE = Annotated Teacher Edition

Block 1 *(45 minutes)*
FOCUS *5 minutes*

❑ **Bellringer,** ATE (GENERAL). This activity has students write their own definitions of the terms *temperature* and *heat.*

MOTIVATE *10 minutes*

❑ **Demonstration,** ATE (GENERAL). This demonstration illustrates the effect of heat on the dispersion of food coloring in a beaker of water. Use the questions in the ATE to guide a follow-up discussion.

Lesson Plan *continued*

TEACH *20 minutes*

❑ **Demonstration,** ATE (GENERAL). This demonstration illustrates how the corrosion of iron is an exothermic reaction.

❑ **Sample Problem A: Calculating the Molar Heat Capacity of a Sample,** SE (GENERAL). This problem demonstrates how to calculate the molar heat capacity of a substance.

CLOSE *10 minutes*

❑ **Reteaching,** ATE (BASIC). Students make analogies to explain the difference between heat and temperature.

❑ **Quiz,** ATE (GENERAL). This assignment has students answer questions about the concepts in this lesson.

❑ **Assessment Worksheet: Section Quiz** (GENERAL)

HOMEWORK

❑ **Reading Skill Builder,** ATE (BASIC). Have students list things that they already know about heat and temperature.

❑ **Practice Sample Problems A,** SE (GENERAL). Calculating the Molar Heat Capacity of a Sample. Assign items 1–4.

❑ **Section Review,** SE (GENERAL). Assign items 1–19.

❑ **Skills Worksheet: Concept Review** (GENERAL)

OTHER RESOURCES

❑ **Teaching Tip,** ATE (ADVANCED). Have interested students learn more about the kinetic-molecular theory by consulting a high school or college physics textbook.

❑ **Homework,** ATE (GENERAL). This assignment provides additional practice problems using calculating molar heat capacity like those in Practice Problem A.

❑ **Using the Table,** ATE (GENERAL). Have students look for trends in Table 1 and use the questions in this feature to help students understand the information presented.

❑ **Focus on Graphing,** SE (GENERAL).

❑ **go.hrw.com**

❑ **www.scilinks.org**

Lesson Plan

Section: Using Enthalpy

Pacing

Regular Schedule	**with lab(s):** NA	**without lab(s):** 1 day
Block Schedule	**with lab(s):** NA	**without lab(s):** ½ day

Objectives

1. Define *thermodynamics*.

2. Calculate the enthalpy change for a given amount of substance for a given change in temperature.

National Science Education Standards Covered

UNIFYING CONCEPTS AND PROCESSES

UCP 1 Systems, order, and organization

UCP 2 Evidence, models, and explanation

UCP 3 Change, constancy, and measurement

PHYSICAL SCIENCE–CHEMICAL REACTIONS

PS 3b Chemical reactions may release or consume energy. Some reactions such as the burning of fossil fuels release large amounts of energy by losing heat and by emitting light. Light can initiate many chemical reactions such as photosynthesis and the evolution of urban smog.

> **KEY**
> **SE** = Student Edition
> **ATE** = Annotated Teacher Edition

Block 2 *(45 minutes)*

FOCUS *5 minutes*

❑ **Bellringer** ATE (GENERAL). This activity has students list examples of objects that have absorbed energy and evidence that the objects have gained energy.

MOTIVATE *10 minutes*

❑ **Demonstration,** ATE (GENERAL). This demonstration shows students how the large molar heat capacity of water prevents a paper cup from burning.

Lesson Plan *continued*

TEACH *25 minutes*

❏ **Teaching Tip,** ATE (GENERAL). Help students understand why absolute enthalpy of a system cannot be known by taking them through this thought exercise.

❏ **Sample Problem B: Calculating Molar Enthalpy Change for Heating,** SE (GENERAL). This problem demonstrates how to calculate molar enthalpy change for heating.

❏ **Sample Problem C: Calculating Molar Enthalpy Change for Cooling,** SE (GENERAL). This problem demonstrates how to calculate molar enthalpy change for cooling.

CLOSE *5 minutes*

❏ **Quiz,** ATE (GENERAL). This assignment has students answer questions about the concepts in this lesson.

❏ **Reteaching,** ATE (BASIC) This activity has students solve for ΔH using two equations.

❏ **Assessment Worksheet: Section Quiz** (GENERAL)

HOMEWORK

❏ **Practice Sample Problems B,** SE (GENERAL). Calculating Molar Enthalpy Change for Heating. Assign items 1–3.

❏ **Practice Sample Problems C,** SE (GENERAL). Calculating Molar Enthalpy Change for Cooling. Assign items 1–3.

❏ **Skills Worksheet: Concept Review** (GENERAL)

❏ **Section Review,** SE (GENERAL). Assign items 1–11.

OTHER RESOURCES

❏ **Homework,** ATE (GENERAL). This assignment gives students additional practice calculating molar enthalpy change for heating. (Sample Problem B).

❏ **Homework,** ATE (GENERAL). This assignment gives students additional practice calculating molar enthalpy change for cooling. (Sample Problem C).

❏ **go.hrw.com**

❏ **www.scilinks.org**

Lesson Plan

Section: Changes in Enthalpy During Chemical Reactions

Pacing

Regular Schedule	**with lab(s):** $3\frac{1}{2}$ days	**without lab(s):** 2 days
Block Schedule	**with lab(s):** 2 days	**without lab(s):** 1 day

Objectives

1. Explain the principle of calorimetry.

2. Use Hess's law and standard enthalpies of formation to calculate ΔH.

National Science Education Standards Covered
UNIFYING CONCEPTS AND PROCESSES

UCP 1 Systems, order, and organization

UCP 2 Evidence, models, and explanation

UCP 3 Change, constancy, and measurement

PHYSICAL SCIENCE—CHEMICAL REACTIONS

PS 3b Chemical reactions may release or consume energy. Some reactions such as the burning of fossil fuels release large amounts of energy by losing heat and by emitting light. Light can initiate many chemical reactions such as photosynthesis and the evolution of urban smog.

> **KEY**
> **SE** = Student Edition
> **ATE** = Annotated Teacher Edition

Block 3 *(45 minutes)*
FOCUS *5 minutes*

❑ **Bellringer** ATE (GENERAL). Students write a short paragraph about food calories and how they relate to nutrition, metabolism, and weight gain/loss.

MOTIVATE *10 minutes*

❑ **Discussion,** ATE (GENERAL). During this discussion, students should determine what endothermic and exothermic mean.

TEACH *35 minutes*

❑ **Transparency,** Bomb Calorimeter. (GENERAL) This transparency illustrates the parts of a bomb calorimeter. (Figure 8)

❑ **Group Activity,** ATE (GENERAL). This activity has students work in groups to calculate the caloric intake and expenditure for one or two people in their group.

Lesson Plan *continued*

❑ **Demonstration,** ATE (GENERAL). This demonstration has students calculate the change in temperature for three reactions and compare them.

❑ **CBL™ Probeware Lab: Energy Content in Foods,** Chapter Resource File (ADVANCED). Students determine perform calorimetry experiments to determine the energy content in various foods.

HOMEWORK

❑ **Section Review,** SE (GENERAL). Assign items 1–3.

OTHER RESOURCES

❑ **Skill Builder,** ATE (ADVANCED). Have students research the different units for energy and find out when each is used.

❑ **Group Activity,** ATE (BASIC). This activity has students work in groups to derive their own analogies of Hess's law.

❑ **go.hrw.com**

❑ **www.scilinks.org**

Block 4 *(45 minutes)*

TEACH *30 minutes*

❑ **Sample Problem D: Calculating a Standard Enthalpy of Formation,** SE (GENERAL). This problem demonstrates how to calculate the heat of a reaction (standard enthalpy of formation).

❑ **Sample Problem E: Calculating a Reaction's Change in Enthalpy,** SE (GENERAL). This problem demonstrates how to calculate a reaction's change in enthalpy.

❑ **Datasheets for In-text Lab: Calorimetry and Hess's Law,** Chapter Resource File (GENERAL). Students will use a calorimeter to determine the heat of reaction for various combinations of an acid and a base.

CLOSE *15 minutes*

❑ **Reteaching,** ATE (BASIC). Students create a concept map using the terms *enthalpy, molar enthalpy change, calorimetry, Hess's law, enthalpy of formation, endothermic, exothermic,* and *nutrition.*

❑ **Quiz,** ATE (GENERAL). This assignment has students answer questions about the concepts in this lesson.

❑ **Assessment Worksheet: Section Quiz** (GENERAL)

HOMEWORK

❑ **Skills Worksheet: Concept Review** (GENERAL) This worksheet reviews the main concepts and problem-solving skills of this section.

❑ **Practice Sample Problems D,** SE (GENERAL). Calculating a Standard Enthalpy of Formation. Assign items 1–2.

Lesson Plan *continued*

❑ **Practice Sample Problems E,** SE (GENERAL). Calculating a Reaction's Change in Enthalpy. Assign items 1–2.

❑ **Homework,** ATE (GENERAL). This assignment has students calculate changes in enthalpy and determine if each reaction is exothermic or endothermic. (Practice Problem E)

❑ **Section Review,** SE (GENERAL). Assign items 4–7.

OTHER RESOURCES

❑ **Skills Worksheet: Problem Solving–Thermochemistry, Sample Problems 1 and 2** (ADVANCED) These worksheets reinforce and extend the concepts and skills developed in Sample Problem E.

❑ **Homework,** ATE (ADVANCED). This assignment has students calculate changes in enthalpy. (Practice Problem D)

❑ **go.hrw.com**

❑ **www.scilinks.org**

Lesson Plan

Section: Order and Spontaneity

Pacing

Regular Schedule   **with lab(s):** NA days   **without lab(s):** 2 days
Block Schedule   **with lab(s):** NA days   **without lab(s):** 1 day

Objectives

1. Define *entropy*, and discuss the factors that influence the sign and magnitude of ΔS for a chemical reaction.

2. Describe *Gibbs energy*, and discuss the factors that influence the sign and magnitude of ΔG.

3. Interpret and indicate whether ΔG values describe spontaneous or nonspontaneous reactions.

National Science Education Standards Covered
UNIFYING CONCEPTS AND PROCESSES

UCP 1 Systems, order, and organization

UCP 2 Evidence, models, and explanation

UCP 3 Change, constancy, and measurement

PHYSICAL SCIENCE—CONSERVATION OF ENERGY AND THE INCREASE IN DISORDER

PS 5d Everything tends to become less organized and less orderly over time. Thus, in all energy transfers, the overall effect is that the energy is spread out uniformly. Examples are the transfer of energy from hotter to cooler objects by conduction, radiation, or convection and the warming of our surroundings when we burn fuels.

KEY
SE = Student Edition
ATE = Annotated Teacher Edition

Block 5 *(45 minutes)*
FOCUS *5 minutes*

❑ **Bellringer,** ATE (GENERAL). Students list examples of both increasing and decreasing disorder.

MOTIVATE *10 minutes*

❑ **Discussion,** ATE (GENERAL). Introduce students to entropy.

TEACH *30 minutes*

❑ **Using the Figure,** ATE (GENERAL). Students cite examples that a chemical reaction has occurred. Then, they cite examples that the entropy of the system has increased.

❑ **Sample Problem F: Hess's Law and Entropy,** SE (GENERAL). This problem demonstrates how to use Hess's Law to calculate entropy.

❑ **Activity,** ATE (BASIC). This activity has students create a graphic organizer to summarize thermodynamic quantities that they have learned.

HOMEWORK

❑ **Reading Skill Builder,** ATE (BASIC). Have students produce an outline of Section 4, using the headings and boldfaced terms.

❑ **Practice Sample Problem F,** SE (GENERAL). Hess's Law and Entropy. Assign items 1–3.

❑ **Homework,** ATE (GENERAL). This assignment has students use Hess's Law to calculate entropy. (Practice Problem F)

OTHER RESOURCES

❑ **go.hrw.com**

❑ **www.scilinks.org**

Block 6 *(45 minutes)*

TEACH *35 minutes*

❑ **Using the Figure,** ATE (GENERAL). Use this feature to explain some aspects of the chemical reaction shown in Figure 14.

❑ **Sample Problem G: Calculating a Change in Gibbs Energy from ΔH and ΔS,** SE (GENERAL). This problem demonstrates how to calculate a change in Gibbs energy from ΔH and ΔS.

❑ **Sample Problem H: Calculating Gibbs Energy Changes Using ΔG Values,** SE (GENERAL). This problem demonstrates how to calculate Gibbs energy changes using ΔG.

CLOSE *10 minutes*

❑ **Quiz,** ATE (GENERAL). This assignment has students answer questions about the concepts in this lesson.

❑ **Assessment Worksheet: Section Quiz** (GENERAL)

Lesson Plan *continued*

HOMEWORK

- ❏ **Practice Sample Problems G,** SE (GENERAL). Calculating a Change in Gibbs Energy from ΔH and ΔS. Assign items 1–3.
- ❏ **Homework,** ATE (GENERAL). This assignment gives students additional practice calculating a change in Gibbs energy from ΔH and ΔS. (Sample Problem G).
- ❏ **Practice Sample Problems H,** SE (GENERAL). Calculating Gibbs Energy Changes Using ΔG Values. Assign items 1–2.
- ❏ **Homework,** ATE (GENERAL). This assignment gives students additional practice calculating a change in Gibbs energy using ΔG. (Sample Problem H).
- ❏ **Skills Worksheet: Concept Review** (GENERAL)
- ❏ **Section Review,** SE (GENERAL). Assign items 1–13.

OTHER RESOURCES

- ❏ **Skill Builder,** ATE (ADVANCED). Have interested students research the three laws of thermodynamics.
- ❏ **Skills Worksheet: Problem Solving–Thermochemistry, Sample Problem** (ADVANCED) These worksheets reinforce and extend the concepts and skills developed in Sample Problem G.
- ❏ **go.hrw.com**
- ❏ **www.scilinks.org**

END OF CHAPTER REVIEW AND ASSESSMENT RESOURCES

- ❏ **Mixed Review,** SE (GENERAL).
- ❏ **Alternate Assessment,** SE (GENERAL).
- ❏ **Technology and Learning,** SE (GENERAL).
- ❏ **Standardized Test Prep,** SE (GENERAL).
- ❏ **Assessment Worksheet: Chapter Test** (GENERAL)
- ❏ **Test Item Listing for ExamView® Test Generator**

Name _______________________________ Class ________________ Date ____________

                    DATASHEETS FOR IN-TEXT LAB

Calorimetry and Hess's Law

A man working for a cleaning firm was told by his employer to pour some old cleaning supplies into a glass container for disposal. Some of the supplies included muriatic (hydrochloric) acid, $HCl(aq)$, and a drain cleaner containing lye, $NaOH(s)$. When the substances were mixed, the container shattered, spilling the contents onto the worker's arms and legs. The worker claims that the hot spill caused burns, and he is, therefore, suing his employer. The employer claims that the worker is lying because the solutions were at room temperature before they were mixed. The employer says that a chemical burn is unlikely because tests after the accident revealed that the mixture had a neutral pH, indicating that the HCl and NaOH were neutralized. The court has asked you to evaluate whether the worker's story is supported by scientific evidence.

Chemicals can be dangerous because of their special storage needs. Acids cannot be stored in metal containers, and organic solvents cannot be kept in plastic containers. Chemicals that are mixed and react are even more dangerous because many reactions release large amounts of heat. Glass, although relatively nonreactive with solutions of pure substances, is heat-sensitive and can shatter if there is a sudden change in temperature due to a reaction. Some glassware, such as Pyrex, is heat-conditioned but can still fracture under extreme heat conditions, especially if scratched.

You will measure the amount of heat released by mixing the chemicals in two ways. First you will break the reaction into steps and measure the heat change of each step. Then you will measure the heat change of the reaction when it takes place all at once. When you are finished, you will be able to use the calorimetry equation from the chapter "Causes of Change" to determine the following:

- the amount of heat evolved during the overall reaction

- the amount of heat for each step

- the amount of heat for the reaction in kilojoules per mole

- whether this heat could have raised the temperature of the water in the solution high enough to cause a burn

OBJECTIVES

Demonstrate proficiency in the use of calorimeters and related equipment.

Relate temperature changes to enthalpy changes.

Determine the heat of reaction for several reactions.

Demonstrate that the heat of reaction can be additive.

Always wear safety goggles and lab apron to protect your eyes and clothing. If you get a chemical in your eyes, immediately flush the chemical out at the eyewash station while calling to your teacher. Know the location of the emergency lab shower and eyewash station and the procedures for using them.

Name _________________________ Class _____________ Date _____________

Calorimetry and Hess's Law *continued*

 **Do not touch any chemicals.** If you get a chemical on your skin or clothing, wash the chemical off at the sink while calling to your teacher. Make sure you carefully read the labels and follow the precautions on all containers of chemicals that you use. If there are no precautions stated on the label, ask your teacher what precautions to follow. Do not taste any chemicals or items used in the laboratory. Never return leftovers to their original container; take only small amounts to avoid wasting supplies.

Call your teacher in the event of a spill. Spills should be cleaned up promptly, according to your teacher's directions.

Acids and bases are corrosive. If an acid or base spills onto your skin or clothing, wash the area immediately with running water. Call your teacher in the event of an acid spill. Acid or base spills should be cleaned up promptly.

Do not heat glassware that is broken, chipped, or cracked. Use tongs or a hot mitt to handle heated glassware and other equipment because hot glassware does not always look hot.

When using a Bunsen burner, confine long hair and loose clothing. If your clothing catches fire, WALK to the emergency lab shower and use it to put out the fire.

MATERIALS

- balance
- distilled water
- glass stirring rod
- graduated cylinder, 100 mL
- HCl solution, 0.50 M
- HCl solution, 1.0 M
- NaOH pellets
- NaOH solution, 1.0 M
- plastic-foam cups (or calorimeters)
- spatula
- thermometer
- watch glass

Optional Equipment

- CBL unit
- graphing calculator with link cable
- Vernier temperature probe

Name _________________________________ Class _______________ Date _____________

Calorimetry and Hess's Law *continued*

Procedure

ADVANCE PREPARATION

1. Put on safety goggles, gloves, and lab apron.

2. If you are not using a plastic-foam cup as a calorimeter, ask your teacher for instructions on using the calorimeter. At various points in the procedure, you will need to measure the temperature of the solution within the calorimeter.

Thermometer Procedure continues on page 39.

CBL AND SENSORS PROCEDURE

3. Connect the CBL to the graphing calculator with the unit-to-unit link cable using the I/O ports located on each unit. Connect the temperature probe to the CH1 port. Turn on the CBL and the graphing calculator. Start the program CHEMBIO on the graphing calculator.

   a. Select option *SET UP PROBES* from the MAIN MENU. Enter 1 for the number of probes. Select the temperature probe from the list. Enter 1 for the channel number. Select *USE STORED* from the CALIBRATION menu.

   b. Select the *COLLECT DATA* option from the MAIN MENU. Select the *TRIGGER* option from the DATA COLLECTION menu.

4. Measure the temperature by gently inserting the Vernier temperature probe into the hole in the calorimeter lid.

Reaction 1: Dissolving NaOH

5. Pour about 100 mL of distilled water into a graduated cylinder. Measure and record the volume of the water to the nearest 0.1 mL. Pour the water into your calorimeter.

6. Using the temperature probe, measure the temperature of the water. Press TRIGGER on the CBL to collect the temperature reading. Record this temperature in your data table. Select *STOP* from the TRIGGER menu on the graphing calculator. Leave the probe in the calorimeter.

7. Select the *COLLECT DATA* option from the MAIN MENU. Select the *TIME GRAPH* option from the DATA COLLECTION menu. Enter 6 for the time between samples, in seconds. Enter 99 for the number of samples (the CBL will collect data for 9.9 min). Press ENTER. Select *USE TIME SETUP* to continue. If you want to change the number of samples or the time between samples, select *MODIFY SETUP*. Enter 0 for *Ymin*, enter 100 for *Ymax*, and enter 5 for *Yscl*.

8. Determine and record the mass of a clean and dry watch glass to the nearest 0.01 g. Remove the watch glass from the balance. While wearing gloves, obtain about 2 g of NaOH pellets, and put them on the watch glass.

Name _______________________________ Class _______________ Date ______________

Calorimetry and Hess's Law *continued*

Use forceps when handling NaOH pellets. Measure and record the mass of the watch glass and the pellets to the nearest 0.01 g. **It is important that this step be done quickly because NaOH is hygroscopic. It absorbs moisture from the air, and its mass increases as long as it remains exposed to the air.**

9. Press ENTER on the graphing calculator to begin collecting the temperature readings for the water in the calorimeter.

10. Immediately place the NaOH pellets in the calorimeter cup, and gently stir the solution with a stirring rod. Place the lid on the calorimeter.

11. When the CBL displays DONE, use the arrow keys to trace the graph. Time in seconds in graphed on the x-axis, and the temperature readings are graphed on the y-axis. Record the highest temperature reading from the CBL in your data table.

12. When the reaction is finished, pour the solution into the container designated by your teacher for disposal of basic solutions.

13. Be sure to clean all equipment and rinse it with distilled water before continuing with the next procedure.

Reaction 2: NaOH and HCl in solution

14. Pour about 50 mL of 1.0 M HCl into a graduated cylinder. Measure and record the volume of the HCl solution to the nearest 0.1 mL. Pour the HCl solution into your calorimeter.

15. Select the *COLLECT DATA* option from the MAIN MENU. Select the *TRIGGER* option from the DATA COLLECTION menu. Using the temperature probe, measure the temperature of the HCl solution. Press TRIGGER on the CBL to collect the temperature reading. Record this temperature in your data table.

16. Pour about 50 mL of 1.0 M NaOH into a graduated cylinder. Measure and record the volume of the NaOH solution to the nearest 0.1 mL. **For this step only, rinse the temperature probe in distilled water.** Using the temperature probe, measure the temperature of the NaOH solution. Press TRIGGER on the CBL to collect the temperature reading. Record this temperature in your data table. Select *STOP* from the TRIGGER menu on the graphing calculator. Put the probe in the calorimeter.

17. Select the *COLLECT DATA* option from the MAIN MENU. Select the *TIME GRAPH* option from the DATA COLLECTION menu. Enter 6 for the time between samples, in seconds. Enter 99 for the number of samples. Press ENTER. Select *USE TIME SETUP* to continue. If you want to change the number of samples or the time between samples, select *MODIFY SETUP*. Enter 0 for *Ymin*, enter 100 for *Ymax*, and enter 5 for *Yscl*. Press ENTER on the calculator to begin collecting temperature readings.

18. Pour the NaOH solution into the calorimeter cup, and stir gently. Place the lid on the calorimeter.

Name _______________________________ Class _____________ Date ___________

Calorimetry and Hess's Law *continued*

19. When the CBL displays DONE, use the arrow keys to trace the graph. Time in seconds in graphed on the x-axis, and the temperature readings are graphed on the y-axis. Record the highest temperature reading from the CBL in your data table.

20. Pour the solution into the container designated by your teacher for disposal of mostly neutral solutions. Clean and rinse all equipment before continuing with the next procedure.

Reaction 3: Solid NaOH and HCl in solution

21. Pour about 100 mL of 0.50 M HCl into a graduated cylinder. Measure and record the volume to the nearest 0.1 mL. Pour the HCl solution into your calorimeter.

22. Select the *COLLECT DATA* option from the MAIN MENU. Select the *TRIG-GER* option from the DATA COLLECTION menu. Using the temperature probe, measure the temperature of the HCl solution. Press TRIGGER on the CBL to collect the temperature reading. Record this temperature in your data table. Select *STOP* from the TRIGGER menu on the graphing calculator.

23. Select the *COLLECT DATA* option from the MAIN MENU. Select the *TIME GRAPH* option from the DATA COLLECTION menu. Enter 6 for the time between samples, in seconds. Enter 99 for the number of samples. Press ENTER. Select *USE TIME SETUP* to continue. If you want to change the number of samples or the time between samples, select *MODIFY SETUP.* Enter 0 for *Ymin*, enter 100 for *Ymax*, and enter 5 for *Yscl*. Press ENTER on the calculator to begin collecting temperature readings.

24. Measure the mass of a clean and dry watch glass, and record it in your data table. Obtain approximately 2 g of NaOH. Place it on the watch glass, and record the total mass to the nearest 0.01 g. **It is important that this step be done quickly because NaOH is hygroscopic.**

25. Press ENTER on the graphing calculator to begin collecting the temperature readings for the water in the calorimeter.

26. Immediately place the NaOH pellets in the calorimeter, and gently stir the solution. Place the lid on the calorimeter.

27. When the CBL displays DONE, use the arrow keys to trace the graph. Time in seconds in graphed on the x-axis, and the temperature readings are graphed on the y-axis. Record the highest temperature reading from the CBL in your data table.

28. When the reaction is finished, pour the solution into the container designated by your teacher for disposal of basic solutions.

29. Clean all apparatus and your lab station. Check with your teacher for the proper disposal procedures. Any excess NaOH pellets should be disposed of in the designated container. Always wash your hands thoroughly after cleaning up the lab area and equipment.

Name _________________________________ Class ________________ Date ______________

Calorimetry and Hess's Law *continued*

THERMOMETER PROCEDURE

3. Measure the temperature by gently inserting the thermometer into the hole in the calorimeter lid. The thermometer takes time to reach the same temperature as the solution inside the calorimeter, so wait to be sure you have an accurate reading. **Thermometers break easily, so be careful with them, and do not use them to stir a solution.**

Reaction 1: Dissolving NaOH

4. Pour about 100 mL of distilled water into a graduated cylinder. Measure and record the volume of the water to the nearest 0.1 mL. Pour the water into your calorimeter. Measure and record the water temperature to the nearest 0.1°C.

5. Determine and record the mass of a clean and dry watch glass to the nearest 0.01 g. Remove the watch glass from the balance. While wearing gloves, obtain about 2 g of NaOH pellets, and put them on the watch glass. Use forceps when handling NaOH pellets. Measure and record the mass of the watch glass and the pellets to the nearest 0.01 g. **It is important that this step be done quickly because NaOH is hygroscopic. It absorbs moisture from the air, and increases its mass as long as it remains exposed to the air.**

6. Immediately place the NaOH pellets in the calorimeter cup, and gently stir the solution with a stirring rod. **Do not stir with a thermometer.** Place the lid on the calorimeter. Watch the thermometer, and record the highest temperature in the data table. When the reaction is finished, pour the solution into the container designated by your teacher for disposal of basic solutions.

7. Be sure to clean all equipment and rinse it with distilled water before continuing with the next procedure.

Reaction 2: NaOH and HCl in solution

8. Pour about 50 mL of 1.0 M HCl into a graduated cylinder. Measure and record the volume of the HCl solution to the nearest 0.1 mL. Pour the HCl solution into your calorimeter. Measure and record the temperature of the HCl solution to the nearest 0.1°C.

9. Pour about 50 mL of 1.0 M NaOH into a graduated cylinder. Measure and record the volume of the NaOH solution to the nearest 0.1 mL. **For this step only, rinse the thermometer in distilled water, and measure the temperature of the NaOH solution in the graduated cylinder to the nearest 0.1°C. Record the temperature in your data table, and then replace the thermometer in the calorimeter.**

10. Pour the NaOH solution into the calorimeter cup, and stir gently. Place the lid on the calorimeter. Watch the thermometer, and record the highest temperature in the data table. When finished with this reaction, pour the solution into the container designated by your teacher for disposal of mostly neutral solutions.

11. Clean and rinse all equipment before continuing with the next procedure.

Holt Chemistry Causes of Change

Name _______________________________ Class _______________ Date _______________

Calorimetry and Hess's Law *continued*

Reaction 3: Solid NaOH and HCl in solution

12. Pour about 100 mL of 0.50 M HCl into a graduated cylinder. Measure and record the volume to the nearest 0.1 mL. Pour the HCl solution into your calorimeter, as shown in Figure B. Measure and record the temperature of the HCl solution to the nearest 0.1°C.

13. Measure the mass of a clean and dry watch glass, and record it in your data table. Obtain approximately 2 g of NaOH. Place it on the watch glass, and record the total mass to the nearest 0.01 g. **It is important that this step be done quickly because NaOH is hygroscopic.**

14. Immediately place the NaOH pellets in the calorimeter, and gently stir the solution. Place the lid on the calorimeter. Watch the thermometer, and record the highest temperature in the data table. When finished with this reaction, pour the solution into the container designated by your teacher for disposal of mostly neutral solutions.

15. Clean all apparatus and your lab station. Check with your teacher for the proper disposal procedures. Any excess NaOH pellets should be disposed of in the designated container. Always wash your hands thoroughly after cleaning up the lab area and equipment.

TABLE 1 TEMPERATURE DATA FOR EACH REACTION

	Reaction 1	Reaction 2	Reaction 3
Mass of empty watch glass	30.15	30.15	
Mass of watch glass with NaOH	32.15	32.16	
Total volumes of liquid(s)	100.0	100.0	100.0
Initial temperature	21.5	22.0	22.0
Final temperature	26.5	28.1	33.0

Analysis

1. Organizing Data Write a balanced chemical equation for each of the three reactions that you performed. (Hint: Be sure to include states of matter for all substances in each equation.)

$NaOH\ (s) \rightarrow NaOH(aq)$

$NaOH(aq) + HCl(aq) \rightarrow H_2O(l) + NaCl(aq)$

$NaOH(s) + HCl(aq) \rightarrow H_2O(l) + NaCl(aq)$

Name ___________________________ Class ______________ Date __________

Calorimetry and Hess's Law *continued*

2. Analyzing Results Find a way to get the equation for the total reaction by adding two of the equations from Analysis item 1 and then canceling out substances that appear in the same form on both sides of the new equation. (Hint: Start with the equation whose product is a reactant in a second equation. Add those two equations together.)

$NaOH\ (s) \rightarrow NaOH(aq)$

$NaOH(aq) + HCl(aq) \rightarrow H_2O(l) + NaCl(aq)$

$NaOH(s) + HCl(aq) \rightarrow H_2O(l) + NaCl(aq)$

3. Explaining Events Explain why a plastic-foam cup makes a better calorimeter than a paper cup does.

A good calorimeter must insulate; any heat created by the reaction should be

absorbed by the water instead of the surroundings. Plastic-foam cups

insulate better than paper cups and therefore make better calorimeters.

4. Organizing Data Calculate the change in temperature (Δt) for each of the reactions.

$\Delta t_1 = 26.5°C - 21.5°C = 5.0°C$

$\Delta t_2 = 28.1°C - 22.0°C = 6.1°C$

$\Delta t_3 = 33.0°C - 22.0°C = 11.0°C$

5. Organizing Data Assuming that the density of the water and the solutions is 1.00 g/mL, calculate the mass, m, of liquid present for each of the reactions.

$m = 100.00\ mL\ H_2O \times 1.00\ g\ H_2O/1\ mL\ H_2O = 100\ g\ H_2O$ for all three reactions

6. Analyzing Results Using the calorimeter equation (Heat $= m \times \Delta t \times c_{p,H_2O}$), calculate the heat released by each reaction. (Hint: Use the specific heat capacity of water in your calculations; $c_{p,H_2O} = 4.180$ J/g·°C.)

heat of reaction 1: $100\ g\ H_2O \times 5.0°C \times 4.180\ J/g·°C = 2100\ J = 2.1\ kJ$

heat of reaction 2: $100\ g\ H_2O \times 6.1°C \times 4.180\ J/g·°C = 2500\ J = 2.5\ kJ$

heat of reaction 3: $100\ g\ H_2O \times 11.0°C \times 4.180\ J/g·°C = 4600\ J = 4.6\ kJ$

Name _________________________ Class ______________ Date ____________

Calorimetry and Hess's Law *continued*

7. Organizing Data Calculate the moles of NaOH used in each of the reactions. (Hint: To find the number of moles in a solution, multiply the volume in liters by the molar concentration.)

moles NaOH for reaction 1:

2.00 g NaOH × 1 ml NaOH/40.00 g NaOH = 5.00×10^{-2} mol NaOH

moles NaOH for reaction 2:

50 mL NaOH × 1L/1000 mL × 1.00 mol NaOH/1L NaOH = 5.00×10^{-2} mol NaOH

moles NaOH for reaction 3:

2.01 g NaOH × 1.00 mol NaOH /40.00 g NaOH = 5.02×10^{-2} mol NaOH

8. Analyzing Results Calculate the ΔH value in terms of kilojoules per mole of NaOH for each of the three reactions.

$\Delta H_1 = -2.1$ kJ/5.00×10^{-2} mol NaOH = -42 kJ/mol NaOH

$\Delta H_2 = -2.5$ kJ/5.00×10^{-2} mol NaOH = -50 kJ/mol NaOH

$\Delta H_3 = -4.6$ kJ/5.00×10^{-2} mol NaOH = -92 kJ/mol NaOH

9. Analyzing Results Using your answer to Analysis item 2 and your knowledge of Hess's law from the chapter "Causes of Change," explain how the enthalpies for the three reactions should be mathematically related.

The sum of the heats of the first two reactions should equal the heat of the third reaction.

10. Analyzing Results Which of the following types of heat of reaction apply to the enthalpies calculated in Analysis item 8: heat of combustion, heat of solution, heat of reaction, heat of fusion, heat of vaporization, and heat of formation?

Reaction 1 involved heat of solution. Reaction 2 involved heat of reaction.

Reaction 3 involved heat of solution and heat of reaction.

Conclusions

11. Evaluating Methods Use your answers from Analysis items 7 and 8 to determine the ΔH value for the reaction of solid NaOH with HCl solution by direct measurement and by indirect calculation.

By direct measurement, ΔH should be -292 kJ/mol.

By indirect calculation, it is also -92 kJ/mol (-50 kJ/mol $- 42$ kJ/mol).

Name _________________________ Class ___________ Date __________

Calorimetry and Hess's Law *continued*

12. **Drawing Conclusions** Third-degree burns can occur if skin comes into contact for more than 4 s with water that is hotter than 60°C (140°F). Suppose someone accidentally poured hydrochloric acid into a glass-disposal container that already contained the drain cleaner NaOH and the container shattered. The solution in the container was approximately 55 g of NaOH and 450 mL of hydrochloric acid solution containing 1.35 mol of HCl (a 3.0 M HCl solution). If the initial temperature of the solutions was 25°C, could a mixture hot enough to cause burns have resulted?

    Molar amount of NaOH:
    55 g NaOH × 1 mol NaOH/40.00 g NaOH = 1.4 mol NaOH

    Molar amount of HCl: 1.35 mol

    Heat of dissolution:
    1.4 mol NaOH × −42kJ/1 mol NaOH = −59 kJ

    Heat of reaction:
    1.35 mol NaOH × −50 kJ/1 mol NaOH = −67.5 kJ

    Total heat of reaction = −59 kJ − 67.5kJ = −126 kJ

    Δt_{H_2O} **− 126 000 J × 1 g·°C/4.180 J × 1/450 g H_2O = 67°C**

    Final temperature = 25°C + 67°C = 92°C (the mixture is likely to cause burns because the temperature would be higher than 60°C)

13. **Applying Conclusions** For the reaction between the drain cleaner and HCl described in item 12, which chemical is the limiting reactant? How many moles of the other reactant remained unreacted?

    HCl is the limiting reactant. There was 0.05 mol NaOH left unreacted.

14. **Evaluating Results** When chemists make solutions from NaOH pellets, they often keep the solution in an ice bath. Explain why.

    The chemists use an ice bath because the heat of solution for NaOH pellets

    is high enough to make the solution dangerously hot.

15. **Evaluating Methods** You have worked with heats of solution for exothermic reactions. Could the same type of procedure be used to determine the temperature changes for endothermic reactions? How would the procedure stay the same? What would change about the procedure and the data?

    The same procedure could be used for endothermic reactions. However, the

    temperature of the water will decrease, and the enthalpy change for the

    reaction will have a positive value.

Name _______________________________ Class _______________ Date __________

Calorimetry and Hess's Law *continued*

16. Drawing Conclusions Which is more stable, solid NaOH or NaOH solution? Explain your answer.

NaOH solution is more stable than solid NaOH. The products of an exothermic

reaction are more stable than the reactants.

Extensions

1. Applying Conclusions When a strongly acidic or basic solution is spilled on a person, the first step is to dilute it by washing the area of the spill with a lot of water. Explain why adding an acid or a base to neutralize the solution immediately is not a good idea.

If acid or base spills are neutralized instead of diluted, the heat of reaction

for the neutralization could cause a heat burn. In addition, the acid or base

could cause a chemical burn.

2. Designing Experiments A chemical supply company is going to ship NaOH pellets to a very humid place, and you have been asked to give advice on packaging. Design a package for the NaOH pellets. Explain the advantages of your package's design and materials. (Hint: Remember that the reaction in which NaOH absorbs moisture from the air is exothermic and that NaOH reacts exothermically with other compounds as well.)

Suggestions for package design will vary. Be sure each design addresses the

dangers of moisture, breakage, and spills.

____

____

____

Skills Practice Lab)   **PROBEWARE LAB**

Energy Content of Foods

Time Required
One lab period (for a two-period lab, have each lab group test all four food samples)

Skills Acquired
- Collecting data
- Experimenting
- Organizing and analyzing data
- Interpreting
- Drawing real-world conclusions

The Scientific Method
- **Analyze the Results** In Analysis questions 1–5, students will compile the data from their experiments and make calculations to determine the caloric content of the foods tested.
- **Draw Conclusions** In Conclusions questions 1–4, students will interpret the data and apply it to the objectives of the experiment.

Teacher's Notes
MATERIALS AND EQUIPMENT
- The food stand can be made using an extra-large paper clip and a small jar lid, such as a baby-food jar lid. Partially straighten the paper clip, then bend a small loop at one end. This loop will cradle food samples. Bend the other end to a V shape—this will be the base. Glue the paper clip into the lid. An advantage of such a stand is its ability to catch pieces of burned food that fall.
- Small soup cans work well. Remove the paper and label the top. Place two holes, large enough to accommodate a stirring rod, near the top. Some teachers prefer to use aluminum beverage cans instead.
- The temperature calibrations that are stored in the DataMate data-collection program will work fine for this experiment. No calibration is necessary for the temperature probes.
- The Vernier stainless steel temperature probe and CBL temperature probe will plug directly into CH1 on the Vernier LabPro or CBL2 interface. If you are using the Vernier direct-connect temperature probe, you will need a DIN-BTA (formerly CBL-DIN) adapter to convert from the 5-pin Din connector to the BTA connector.

Energy Content of Foods *continued*

SAFETY CAUTIONS

- Be sure to remove all sharp edges from cans.

- Because peanuts and cashew nuts release very large amounts of heat as they burn, you may want to have your students use 100 mL portions of cold water when testing these foods.

- Some students may be allergic to peanuts. Before proceeding with this activity, poll your students to determine if anyone in the class is allergic to peanuts. If any are, do not allow any students to perform the part involving peanuts. Have students answer Conclusions question 2 for cashews instead of peanuts.

Graphing Calculator and Sensors
TIPS AND TRICKS

- Students should have the DataMate program loaded on their graphing calculators. Refer to Appendix B of Vernier's *Chemistry with Calculators* for instructions.

- Not all models of TI graphing calculators have the same amount of memory. If possible, instruct students to clear all calculator memory before loading the DataMate program.

TECHNIQUES TO DEMONSTRATE

When viewing graphs on the calculator, students should use the arrow keys to trace the data points on the graph.

If students wish to see the data for both food samples on the same graph, instruct them to store the first data set before beginning the second food sample. From the Main Screen of DataMate, the Store Latest Run feature can be found under the Tools menu. The program will only permit storing up to two runs. If more than one sensor is used at a time, the Store Latest Run feature will not work.

Experimental Setup
TIPS AND TRICKS

- Supply students with water that is 15°C to 18°C to achieve best results.

- Perform this experiment in a fume hood or in a well-ventilated classroom.

Answers
CONCLUSIONS

1. Cashews and peanuts have the highest energy content. Marshmallows and popcorn have the lowest.

2. Calories in a 50.0 g package of peanuts:
   $(12.0 \text{ kJ/g})(50.0 \text{ g})(1 \text{ Cal} / 4.18 \text{ kJ}) = 155 \text{ Cal}$

Energy Content of Foods *continued*

3. The two foods with a high fat content, cashews and peanuts, have a much higher energy content than those with a high carbohydrate content (nearly double the energy content).

4. On average, peanuts have the highest energy content per gram, followed by cashews.

EXTENSIONS

1. Nuts of any kind would be a good energy source for the physical demands involved.

2. Answers should discuss the possible loss of heat between the burner and the thermometer and possible improvements to keep that loss to near zero—for instance, insulating the space between the burner and the water to prevent heat loss.

3. The nutrition labels for peanuts and popcorn are accurate. The labels for marshmallows and cashews are not accurate. The marshmallow label indicates a higher Calorie and fat content than is likely. The label for cashews indicates a fat and Calorie content that is too low.

MARSHMALLOWS (Corrected)

Nutrition Facts	
Serving Size 1 ounce	
Servings Per Container 6	
Amount per serving	
Calories 90	Calories from Fat 0
	% Daily Value
Total Fat 0g	*%
Saturated Fat 0g	*%
Cholesterol 0mg	*%
Sodium 13mg	*%
Total Carbohydrate 23g	8%
Dietary Fiber 0g	*%
Sugars 5.9g	
Protein 0.1g	
***Less than 1% of US RDA**	

PEANUTS (oil roasted w/salt)

Nutrition Facts	
Serving Size 1 ounce	
Servings Per Container 16	
Amount per serving	
Calories 165	Calories from Fat 125
	% Daily Value
Total Fat 14g	70%
Saturated Fat 1.9g	35%
Cholesterol 0mg	0%
Sodium 122mg	18%
Total Carbohydrate 6g	6%
Dietary Fiber 3g	4%
Sugars 3g	
Protein 8g	

Energy Content of Foods *continued*

CASHEWS (oil roasted w/salt) (Corrected)

Nutrition Facts	
Serving Size 1 ounce	
Servings Per Container 16	
Amount per serving	
Calories 163	Calories from Fat 26
	% Daily Value
Total Fat 13.7g	**69%**
Saturated Fat 2.7g	**48%**
Cholesterol 0mg	**0%**
Sodium 177mg	**26%**
Total Carbohydrate 8g	**10%**
Dietary Fiber 1g	**1%**
Sugars 7g	
Protein 5g	

POPCORN (air-popped, no salt)

Nutrition Facts	
Serving Size 1 cup	
Servings Per Container 8	
Amount per serving	
Calories 30	Calories from Fat 0
	% Daily Value
Total Fat 0.3g	*%
Saturated Fat 0g	*%
Cholesterol 0mg	**0%**
Sodium 0mg	*%
Total Carbohydrate 6g	**2%**
Dietary Fiber 1g	**4%**
Sugars 2g	
Protein 0g	
***Less than 1% of US RDA**	

DATA TABLES WITH SAMPLE DATA

DATA TABLE 1

Food sample 1:			
Initial mass of food sample and holder:	14.04 g		
Mass of empty can:	41.31 g	Mass of can and water:	90.69 g

DATA TABLE 2

Food sample 1:			
T_1: 15.4°C	T_2: 52.9°C	final mass of sample and holder:	13.36

DATA TABLE 3

Food sample 1:			
Mass of water heated:	49.38 g	Temperature change, ΔT:	37.5 °C
Mass of food burned:	0.68 g	Heat, q:	7.74 kJ
Energy content of food sample:			11.4 kJ/g

CLASS AVERAGES

Marshmallows	Peanuts	Cashews	Popcorn
5.2 kJ/g	11.8 kJ/g	11.5 kJ/g	6.7 kJ/g

Name _______________________________ Class _______________ Date _______________

PROBEWARE LAB

Energy Content of Foods

You are a lab technician working for NASA. Recently you were given the job of deciding what type of foods should be included in the next space mission. Four food types have been selected as possible snacks for the astronauts. You need to determine which of these four food choices has the highest energy content while adding the least amount of mass to the mission.

Your team will test two of the food types using a method known as calorimetry. During this process, you will burn a food sample positioned below a can containing a given amount of cold water. The water temperature will be monitored during the experiment using a temperature probe. By calculating the temperature change of the water, you will determine how much energy was released when the food sample burned.

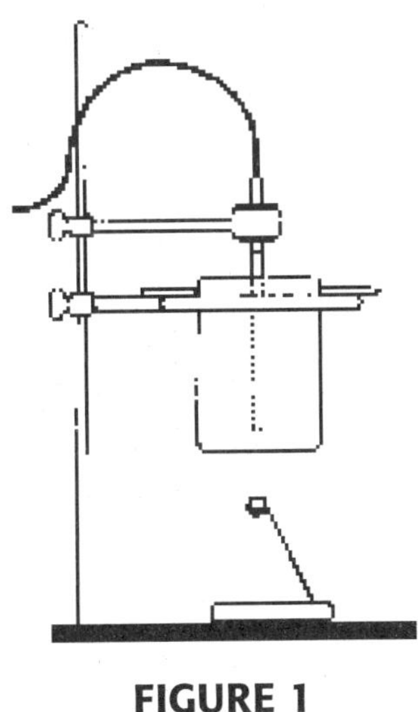

FIGURE 1

OBJECTIVES

- **Measure** temperature changes.
- **Calculate** energy changes using specific heat.
- **Infer** the energy content of food.
- **Relate** energy content to types of food.
- **Evaluate** whether the nutrition labels are accurate.

MATERIALS

- can, small
- food samples (2)
- matches
- water, cold
- wooden splint

Name _________________________ Class _______________ Date _____________

Energy Content of Foods *continued*

EQUIPMENT

- food holder (see **Figure 1**)
- graduated cylinder, 100 mL
- LabPro or CBL2 interface
- stirring rods (2)
- ring stand and 4-inch ring
- TI graphing calculator
- utility clamp and slit stopper
- Vernier temperature probe

SAFETY     

- Wear safety goggles when working around chemicals, acids, bases, flames, or heating devices. Contents under pressure may become projectiles and cause serious injury.

- Secure loose clothing, and remove dangling jewelry. Do not wear open-toed shoes or sandals in the lab.

- Wear an apron or lab coat to protect your clothing when working with chemicals.

- In order to avoid burns, wear heat-resistant gloves whenever instructed to do so.

- If you are unsure of whether an object is hot, do not touch it.

- Avoid wearing hair spray or hair gel on lab days.

- Whenever possible, use an electric hot plate as a heat source instead of an open flame.

- Never return unused chemicals to the original container; follow instructions for proper disposal.

Procedure

EQUIPMENT PREPARATION

1. Obtain and wear goggles.

2. Plug the temperature probe into Channel 1 of the LabPro or CBL 2 interface. Use the link cable to connect the TI graphing calculator to the interface. Firmly press in the cable ends.

3. Turn on the calculator, and start the DATAMATE program. Press `CLEAR` to reset the program.

4. Set up the calculator and interface for the temperature probe.

    a. Select SETUP from the main screen.

    b. If the calculator displays a temperature probe in CH 1, proceed directly to Step 5. If it does not, continue with this step to set up your sensor manually.

    c. Press `ENTER` to select CH 1.

    d. Select TEMPERATURE from the SELECT SENSOR menu.

    e. Select the temperature probe you are using (in °C) from the TEMPERATURE menu.

Name _________________________ Class _____________ Date ___________

Energy Content of Foods *continued*

5. Set up the data-collection mode.

   a. To select MODE, press ▲ once and press ENTER.

   b. Select TIME GRAPH from the SELECT MODE menu.

   c. Select CHANGE TIME SETTINGS from the TIME GRAPH SETTINGS menu.

   d. Enter "6" as the time between samples in seconds.

   e. Enter "100" as the number of samples. The length of the data collection will be 10 minutes.

   f. Select OK to return to the setup screen.

   g. Select OK again to return to the main screen.

6. Obtain a piece of one of the two foods assigned to you and a food holder like the one shown in **Figure 1.** Find and record the initial mass of the food sample and food holder. **CAUTION:** *Do not eat or drink in the laboratory.*

7. Determine and record the mass of an empty can. Obtain cold water from your teacher, and add 50 mL of it to the can. Determine and record the mass of the can and water.

8. Set up the apparatus as shown in **Figure 1.** Use a ring and stirring rod to suspend the can about 2.5 cm (1 in.) above the food sample. Use a utility clamp to suspend the temperature probe in the water. The probe should not touch the bottom of the can. Remember that the temperature probe must be in the water for at least 30 seconds before you complete Step 9.

DATA TABLE 1

Food sample 1:		
Initial mass of food sample and holder:		
Mass of empty can:		Mass of can and water:
Food sample 2:		
Initial mass of food sample and holder:		
Mass of empty can:		Mass of can and water:

DATA COLLECTION

9. Select START to begin collecting data. Record the initial temperature of the water, T_1, in Data Table 2 (round to the nearest 0.1°C). **Note:** You can monitor temperature in the upper-right corner of the real-time graph displayed on the calculator screen. Remove the food sample from under the can, and use a wooden splint to light it. Quickly place the burning food sample directly under the center of the can. Allow the water to be heated until the food sample stops burning.

10. Continue stirring the water until the temperature stops rising. Record this maximum temperature, T_2. Data collection will stop after 10 minutes (or press the STOP key to stop *before* 10 minutes have elapsed).

11. Determine and record the final mass of the food sample and food holder.

Name _________________________________ Class ______________ Date __________

Energy Content of Foods *continued*

12. To confirm the initial (T_1) and final (T_2) values you recorded earlier, examine the data points along the curve on the displayed graph. As you move the cursor right or left, the time (X) and temperature (Y) values of each data point are displayed below the graph.

13. Press ENTER to return to the main screen. Select START to repeat the data collection for the second food sample. Use a new 50 mL portion of cold water. Repeat Steps 6–12.

14. When you are done, place burned food, used matches, and partially burned wooden splints in the container provided by the teacher.

DATA TABLE 2

Food sample 1:				
T_1:		T_2:	Final mass of sample and holder:	
Food sample 2:				
T_1:		T_2:	Final mass of sample and holder:	

Analysis

1. Organizing data Find the mass of water heated for each sample. __________

____

2. Organizing data Find the change in temperature of the water, ΔT, for each

sample. ____

____

3. Organizing data Find the mass (in g) of each food sample burned. _________

____

4. Analyzing Results Calculate the heat absorbed by the water, q, using the equation

$$q = C_p m \Delta T$$

where q is heat, C_p is the specific heat, m is the mass of water, and ΔT is the change in temperature. For water, C_p is 4.18 J/g°C. Convert your final answer

to units of kJ. ______________________________________

____

____

Name _________________________________ Class _______________ Date ___________

Energy Content of Foods *continued*

5. Analyzing Results Use the results of the previous two steps to calculate the

energy content (in kJ/g) of each food sample. _______________________________

____

DATA TABLE 3

Food sample 1:					
Mass of water heated:		g	Temperature change, ΔT:		°C
Mass of food burned:		g	Heat, q:		kJ
Energy content of food sample:					kJ/g
Food sample 2:					
Mass of water heated:		g	Temperature change, ΔT:		°C
Mass of food burned:		g	Heat, q:		kJ
Energy content of food sample:					kJ/g

Conclusions

1. Evaluating results Record your results and the results of other groups in the
Class Results Table below. Which food had the highest energy content? Which

had the lowest energy content? ____

____

CLASS RESULTS TABLE

Marshmallows	Peanuts	Cashews	Popcorn
kJ/g	kJ/g	kJ/g	kJ/g
kJ/g	kJ/g	kJ/g	kJ/g
kJ/g	kJ/g	kJ/g	kJ/g
kJ/g	kJ/g	kJ/g	kJ/g
kJ/g	kJ/g	kJ/g	kJ/g

Average for each food type:

kJ/g	kJ/g	kJ/g	kJ/g

2. Evaluating results Food energy is often expressed in a unit called a Calorie
(or dietary calorie). There are 4.18 kJ in one Calorie. Based on the class
average for popcorn, calculate the number of Calories in a 50.0 g package

of popcorn. ____

____

Name _________________________________ Class _______________ Date _______________

Energy Content of Foods *continued*

3. **Evaluating results** Two of the foods in the experiment have a high fat content (peanuts and cashews), and two have a high carbohydrate content (marshmallows and popcorn). From your results, what generalization can you make

about the relative energy content of fats and carbohydrates? _______________

____

____

4. **Evaluating results** Based on the data you and your classmates collected, which of the four foods tested would you suggest to send on the NASA space mission?

____

____

Extensions

1. **Applying results** If you were packing for a mountain hike, what kind of

snacks would you bring along? Why? _______________________________

____

____

2. **Critiquing methods** Was all of the heat given off by the burning food sample transferred to the water in the can? How could this experiment be improved to account for all the heat given off when the food sample was burned?

____

____

____

____

3. **Applying results** Listed on the following page are possible nutrition labels for each of the food samples that you tested. Based on the data you and your classmates obtained in this lab, determine which of these labels is accurate and which is not. If you find a label to be incorrect, explain your reasoning.

____

____

____

____

Name _________________________ Class _______________ Date _____________

Energy Content of Foods *continued*

MARSHMALLOWS

Nutrition Facts

Serving Size 1 ounce

Servings Per Container 6

Amount per serving

Calories 260	Calories from Fat 160
	% Daily Value
Total Fat 18g	**13%**
Saturated Fat 5g	**27%**
Cholesterol 0mg	**0%**
Sodium 260mg	**11%**
Total Carbohydrate 23g	**8%**
Dietary Fiber 1g	**11%**
Sugars 18g	
Protein 1g	

PEANUTS

Nutrition Facts

Serving Size 1 ounce

Servings Per Container 16

Amount per serving

Calories 165	Calories from Fat 125
	% Daily Value
Total Fat 14g	**20%**
Saturated Fat 1.9g	**10%**
Cholesterol 0mg	**0%**
Sodium 122mg	**5%**
Total Carbohydrate 5g	**2%**
Dietary Fiber 1g	**4%**
Sugars 2g	
Protein 8g	

CASHEWS

Nutrition Facts

Serving Size 1 ounce

Servings Per Container 16

Amount per serving

Calories 80	Calories from Fat 26
	% Daily Value
Total Fat 3g	**4%**
Saturated Fat 0.5g	**3%**
Cholesterol 0mg	**0%**
Sodium 177mg	**7%**
Total Carbohydrate 8g	**3%**
Dietary Fiber 2g	**8%**
Sugars 2g	
Protein 5g	

POPCORN

Nutrition Facts

Serving Size 1 cup

Servings Per Container 8

Amount per serving

Calories 30	Calories from Fat 0
	% Daily Value
Total Fat 0.3g	***%**
Saturated Fat 0g	***%**
Cholesterol 0mg	**0%**
Sodium 0mg	***%**
Total Carbohydrate 6g	**2%**
Dietary Fiber 1g	**4%**
Sugars 2g	
Protein 0g	
***Less than 1% of US RDA**	

Answer Key

Concept Review: Energy Transfer

1. physical
2. higher, lower, heat, temperature
3. intensive, extensive
4. enthalpy
5. Kelvin
6. Celsius
7. 273.15 K
8. the same
9. joules
10. -200
11. 273.15
12. $q = Cn\Delta T$ $\Delta T = 40.0°C - 10.0°C$
    $= 30.0°C$ is equal to 30.0 K
    75.3 J/K·mol $\times$ 180.0 g H_2O/18.02
    g/mol H_2O $\times$ 30.0 K $= 2.26 \times 10^4$ J
13. $q = Cn\Delta T$ $\Delta T = 75.0°C - 15.0°C$
    $= 60.0°C$ is equal to 60.0 K
    24.2 J/K·mol $\times$ 250.0 g Al/26.98 g/mol
    Al $\times$ 60.0 K $= 1.35 \times 10^4$ J
14. $q = Cn\Delta T$ $\Delta T = 80.0°C - 25.0°C$
    $= 55.0°C$ is equal to 55.0 K
    11.1 J/K · mol $\times$ 68.0 g Sn/118.71g/mol
    Sn $\times$ 55.0 K $= 350.$ J
15. $q = Cn\Delta T;$ $q = 29.1$ J/K mol $\times$ 1.44
    mole $\times$ 45 K; $q = 1894$ J

Concept Review: Using Enthalpy

1. enthalpy, change, molar
2. same, molar heat capacity, temperature
   $C\Delta T$
3. positive, endothermic, negative, exothermic
4. thermodynamics
5. $\Delta H = C\Delta T$
   $\Delta T = 17.0°C - 90.0°C = -73.0°C$
   $= -73.0$ K
   $\Delta H = 75.3$ J/K·mol $\times -73.0$ K
   $= -5.50$ kJ/mol
6. $\Delta H = C\Delta T$
   $\Delta T = 71.0°C - 18.0°C = +53.0°C$
   $= +53.0$ K
   $\Delta H = 75.3$ J/K·mol $\times +53.0$ K
   $= +4.00$ kJ/mol

Concept Review: Changes in Enthalpy During Reactions

1. heat, temperature, reactants, products, 25, 298.15, moles, standard enthalpy of formation
2. In a bomb calorimeter a sample is ignited in high-pressure oxygen contained in a heavy steel chamber surrounded by water. The energy as heat from the combustion is absorbed by the surrounding water and by other parts of the colorimeter. The water and the other parts of the calorimeter have known specific heats, so a measured temperature increase can be used to calculate energy released and then the enthalpy change. Adiabatic calorimeters use an insulating vessel instead of a water bath to absorb the energy generated by a reaction. Adiabatic calorimetry is used for reactions that are not ignited, such as for reactions in aqueous solution.
3. The overall enthalpy change in a reaction is equal to the sum of the enthalpy changes for the individual steps in the process.
4. $\Delta H = \Delta H$ of products $- \Delta H$ of reactants
   $\Delta H = (2(-92.3$ kJ/mol$) + (+30.9$ kJ/mol$)) - ((0) + 2(-36.4$ kJ/mol$))$
   $= 80.9$ kJ/mol exothermic
5. $\Delta H = \Delta H$ of products $- \Delta H$ of reactants
   $\Delta H = ((-634.9$ kJ/mol$) + (-393.5$ kJ/mol$)) - (-1206.9$ kJ/mol$) =$
   $+178.5$ kJ/mol endothermic

Concept Review: Order and Spontaneity

1. entropy, energy
2. standard entropy
3. S, J/K·mol
4. Gibbs energy, H-TS
5. positive

6. increases
7. Gases
8. Gases
9. absolute zero
10. products, reactants
11. negative
12. disorder
13. negative
14. decrease
15. endothermic
16. positive
17. minimum
18. decrease
19. spontaneous
20. negative, exothermic, increase
21. positive, endothermic, decrease
22. entropy
23. higher
24. small, enthalpy
25. $\Delta S = $ sum of $S^0_{(products)} - $ sum of $S^0_{(reactants)}$
$\Delta S = ((83.4 \text{ J/K·mol}) + (130.7 \text{ J/K·mol})) - ((41.6 \text{ J/K·mol}) + 2(70.0 \text{ J/K·mol})) = +32.5 \text{ J/K·mol}$
26. $\Delta S = $ sum of $S^0_{(products)} - $ sum of $S^0_{(reactants)}$
$\Delta S = (2(70.0 \text{ J/K·mol}) + 2(152.2 \text{ J/K·mol})) - (4(198.6 \text{ J/K·mol}) + (205.1 \text{ J/K·mol})) = -555.1 \text{ J/K·mol}$
27. $\Delta H = (2(-285.8 \text{ kJ/mol}) + 0) - 2(-187.8 \text{ kJ/mol}) = -196.0 \text{ kJ/mol}$
$\Delta S = (2(70.0 \text{ J/K·mol}) + 205.1 \text{ J/K·mol}) - 2(109.6 \text{ J/K·mol}) = 125.9 \text{ J/K·mol}$
$\Delta G = \Delta H - T\Delta S$:
$T = 25°C = 298 \text{ K}$
$\Delta G = (-196.0 \text{ kJ/mol}) - (298 \text{ K} \times 125.9 \text{ J/K·mol}) = -233.5 \text{ kJ/mol}$
spontaneous
28. $\Delta H = ((-634.9 \text{ kJ/mol}) + (-393.5 \text{ kJ/mol})) - (-1206.9 \text{ kJ/mol}) = +178.5 \text{ kJ/mol}$
$\Delta S = (38.2 \text{ J/K·mol} + 213.8 \text{ J/K·mol}) - 92.9 \text{ J/K·mol} = 159.1 \text{ J/K·mol}$
$\Delta G = \Delta H - T\Delta S$:
$T = 25°C = 298 \text{ K}$
$\Delta G = (+178.5 \text{ kJ/mol}) - (298 \text{ K} \times 159.1 \text{ J/K·mol}) = +131.1 \text{ kJ/mol}$
nonspontaneous

Additional Problems

THERMOCHEMISTRY

1. -260.8 kJ/mol
2. -385.9 kJ/mol
3. $-390.$ kJ/mol
4. -492.3 kJ/mol
5. -107.6 kJ/mol
6. -121.8 kJ/mol
7. -384.9 kJ/mol
8. 74.2 kJ/mol
9. -169.0 kJ/mol
10. **a.** $CH_4(g) + 2O_2(g) \rightarrow CO_2(g) + 2H_2O(g)$
$C_3H_8(g) + 5O_2(g) \rightarrow 3CO_2(g) + 4H_2O(g)$
   b. for methane: $\Delta H = -802.2$ kJ/mol
for propane: $\Delta H = -2043$ kJ/mol
   c. $\text{output}_{methane} = -4.998 \times 10^4$ kJ/kg
$\text{output}_{propane} = -4.632 \times 10^4$ kJ/kg
Methane yields more heat per mass.
11. -132.7 kJ/mol
12. -7171.4 kJ/mol
13. -141.1 kJ/mol
14. 20.2 kJ/mol
15. -285 kJ/mol·K
16. **a.** 786.8 kJ/mol
   b. -36 kJ/mol
   c. 2154 kJ/mol
   d. -496 kJ/mol
   e. 1346.4 kJ/mol

Answer Key

Quiz—Section: Energy Transfer

1. a	**6.** b
2. c	**7.** c
3. b	**8.** a
4. c	**9.** b
5. d	**10.** c

Quiz—Section: Using Enthalpy

1. c	**6.** d
2. a	**7.** a
3. a	**8.** c
4. c	**9.** b
5. b	**10.** b

Quiz—Section: Changes in Enthalpy During Reactions

1. c	**6.** a
2. b	**7.** a
3. b	**8.** d
4. c	**9.** c
5. c	**10.** d

Quiz—Section: Order and Spontaneity

1. b	**6.** b
2. a	**7.** a
3. d	**8.** c
4. a	**9.** b
5. a	**10.** c

Chapter Test

1. d	**11.** a
2. d	**12.** b
3. c	**13.** c
4. a	**14.** d
5. b	**15.** a
6. c	**16.** a
7. a	**17.** b
8. a	**18.** b
9. b	**19.** c
10. b	**20.** b

21. Temperature is a measure of the average kinetic energy of a substance. Heat is the total thermal energy of the substance.

22. The temperature is necessary because the entropy factor of the free energy equation depends on temperature in kelvins.

23. $\Delta G = \Delta H - T\Delta S$
$\Delta G = 23 \text{ kJ} - (298 \text{ K} \times -130 \text{ J/ K}) = 23 \text{ kJ} - (-38740 \text{ J})$
$\Delta G = 61.7 \text{ kJ}$

24. $\Delta H = \text{moles Ag} \times C \times \Delta T = (175 \text{ g}/107.9 \text{ g/mol}) \times 25.3 \text{ J/K·mol} \times (40 - 22.5 \text{ K})$
$\Delta H = 1.62 \text{ mol} \times 25.3 \text{ J/K·mol} \times 17.5 \text{ K}$
$\Delta H = 718 \text{ J}$

25. $\Delta H = \Delta T \times C \times \text{moles of water} = (74.0 - 25.0°\text{C}) \times 75.3 \text{ J/ K·mol} \times (2500 \text{ g}/18 \text{ g/mol})$

$\Delta H = 49.0°\text{C} \times 75.3 \text{ J/ K·mol} \times 138.9 \text{ mol}$
$\Delta H = 512 \text{ kJ}$

Causes of Change

MULTIPLE CHOICE

1. Enthalpy is the
   a. heat of formation at constant pressure.
   b. heat of combustion at constant pressure.
   c. energy of a system at constant pressure.
   d. change in energy of a system at constant pressure.
   Answer: C   Difficulty: I   Section: 1   Objective: 1

2. The Greek letter Δ stands for
   a. "heat stored in."   c. "rate of."
   b. "mass of."   d. "change in."
   Answer: D   Difficulty: I   Section: 1   Objective: 1

3. Which of the following is a measure of the average kinetic energy of the particles in a sample of matter?
   a. chemical kinetics   c. reaction rate
   b. thermochemistry   d. temperature
   Answer: D   Difficulty: I   Section: 1   Objective: 2

4. Which of the following best describes temperature?
   a. heat absorbed or released in a chemical or physical change
   b. a measure of the average kinetic energy of the particles in a sample of matter
   c. heat energy
   d. energy of change
   Answer: B   Difficulty: I   Section: 1   Objective: 2

5. How is a Celsius temperature converted to kelvins?
   a. by adding 273.15   c. by dividing by 273.15
   b. by subtracting 273.15   d. by multiplying by 273.15
   Answer: A   Difficulty: I   Section: 1   Objective: 2

6. The greater the kinetic energy of the particles in a sample of matter,
   a. the higher the temperature is.
   b. the lower the temperature is.
   c. the more heat the sample will absorb.
   d. the less heat flows away from the sample.
   Answer: A   Difficulty: I   Section: 1   Objective: 2

7. In the expression $q = nc\Delta T$, what do q and n represent?
   a. heat and number of particles   c. heat capacity and moles of particles
   b. heat and moles of particles   d. enthalpy and moles of particles
   Answer: B   Difficulty: I   Section: 1   Objective: 3

8. A 111.6 g sample of iron (MW = 55.8) was heated from 0°C to 20°C. It absorbed 1004 J of energy. What is the molar heat capacity of iron?
   a. 50.2 J/K·mol   c. 502 J/K·mol
   b. 251 J/K·mol   d. 25.1 J/K·mol
   Answer: D   Difficulty: III   Section: 1   Objective: 3

9. How much energy does a mercury (MW = 200.6) sample gain if its molar heat capacity is 27.8 J/K·mol, its mass is 2.01 g, and it is heated from 10.0°C to 40.0°C?
   a. 0.120 J/g   c. 8.34 J
   b. 0.120 J   d. 8.34 J/g
   Answer: C   Difficulty: III   Section: 1   Objective: 3

10. The study of all energy changes is called
    a. thermodynamics.
    b. enthalpy.
    c. entropy.
    d. temperature.

    Answer: A   Difficulty: I   Section: 2   Objective: 1

11. The topics covered by the study of thermodynamics include
    a. energy changes during heating.
    b. energy changes during chemical reactions.
    c. color changes during chemical reactions.
    d. Both a and b

    Answer: D   Difficulty: I   Section: 2   Objective: 1

12. What is the molar enthalpy change when a block of aluminum is cooled by 20 K. The
    molar heat capacity of aluminum is 24.2 J/K·mol?
    a. 24.2 J/mol
    b. 484 J/mol
    c. -24.2 J/mol
    d. -484 J/mol

    Answer: D   Difficulty: II   Section: 1   Objective: 2

13. What is the molar enthalpy change when a 1 kg block of aluminum is heated by 20 K.
    The molar heat capacity of aluminum is 24.2 J/K·mol?
    a. 24.2 J/mol
    b. 484 J/mol
    c. -24.2 J/mol
    d. -484 J/mol

    Answer: B   Difficulty: II   Section: 1   Objective: 2

14. If the enthalpy of 1 mol of a compound decreases by 328 J when it is cooled by 10 K, what
    is its molar heat capacity?
    a. -32.8 J/K·mol
    b. 32.8 J/K·mol
    c. 328 J/mol
    d. 32.8 J/mol

    Answer: B   Difficulty: II   Section: 1   Objective: 2

15. What is the standard thermodynamic temperature?
    a. 25°C
    b. 25 K
    c. -24.2 J/mol
    d. -484 J/K·mol

    Answer: A   Difficulty: I   Section: 3   Objective: 1

16. In a calorimeter, the energy content of a substance is calculated from measurement of the
    temperature change in a known mass of
    a. iron.
    b. air.
    c. water.
    d. steel.

    Answer: C   Difficulty: I   Section: 3   Objective: 1

17. For an exothermic reaction, the products
    a. are at the same energy level as the reactants.
    b. have no energy.
    c. are at a lower energy level than the reactants.
    d. are at a higher energy level than the reactants.

    Answer: C   Difficulty: I   Section: 3   Objective: 2

18. The total enthalpy of the products in a reaction is 458 kJ, and the total enthalpy of the
    reactants is 658 kJ. What is ΔH for the reaction?
    a. –1116 kJ
    b. –200 kJ
    c. +200 kJ
    d. +1116 kJ

    Answer: B   Difficulty: III   Section: 3   Objective: 2

19. The total enthalpy of the products in a reaction is 0 kJ, and the total enthalpy of the reactants is 100 kJ. What is ΔH for the reaction?
    a. –393.5 kJ
    b. –100 kJ
    c. 0 kJ
    d. +100 kJ

    Answer: B   Difficulty: III   Section: 3   Objective: 2

20. The enthalpy of formation of a compound is –612 kJ/mol, and the products of its combustion have a total enthalpy of formation of –671 kJ. What is the enthalpy of combustion of this compound?
    a. –59 kJ/mol
    b. –40 kJ/mol
    c. +40 kJ/mol
    d. +59 kJ/mol

    Answer: A   Difficulty: III   Section: 3   Objective: 2

21. The enthalpy of a reaction for a chemical change can be determined by
    a. multiplying the total enthalpies of the products and reactants.
    b. subtracting the total enthalpy of the reactants from that of the products.
    c. subtracting the total enthalpy of the products from that of the reactants.
    d. adding the total enthalpies of the products and reactants.

    Answer: B   Difficulty: I   Section: 3   Objective: 2

22. Compounds whose enthalpies of formation are highly negative
    a. do not exist.
    b. are very unstable.
    c. are somewhat stable.
    d. are very stable.

    Answer: D   Difficulty: I   Section: 3   Objective: 2

23. Which of the following is a measure of the disorder in a system?
    a. entropy
    b. enthalpy
    c. kinetic energy
    d. temperature

    Answer: A   Difficulty: I   Section: 4   Objective: 1

24. Compared with a single gas, a mixture of gases is
    a. more disordered.
    b. less disordered.
    c. equally disordered.
    d. less favorable.

    Answer: A   Difficulty: I   Section: 4   Objective: 1

25. Entropy decreases as a result of
    a. a decrease in pressure.
    b. a decrease in temperature.
    c. agitation.
    d. an increase in temperature.

    Answer: B   Difficulty: I   Section: 4   Objective: 1

26. What is the value of ΔG at 300 K for a reaction in which ΔH = –150 kJ/mol and ΔS = +2.00 kJ/mol·K?
    a. –750 kJ/mol
    b. –450 kJ/mol
    c. +750 kJ/mol
    d. +450 kJ/mol

    Answer: A   Difficulty: III   Section: 4   Objective: 2

27. Which expression defines the change in Gibbs energy?
    a. $\Delta H + T\Delta G$
    b. $\Delta H + T\Delta S$
    c. $\Delta H - T\Delta S$
    d. $\Delta S - T\Delta H$

    Answer: C   Difficulty: I   Section: 4   Objective: 2

28. Entropy plays a larger role in determining the Gibbs energy of reactions that take place at
    a. high temperatures.
    b. low temperatures.
    c. high pressures.
    d. low pressures.

    Answer: A   Difficulty: I   Section: 4   Objective: 2

29. Which depends only on the initial and final states of a reaction, rather than on the intermediate processes?
    a. ΔH only
    b. ΔS only
    c. both ΔH and ΔS
    d. $T\Delta S$
    Answer: C   Difficulty: I   Section: 4   Objective: 2

30. A reaction occurs spontaneously when ΔG is
    a. positive.
    b. negative.
    c. zero.
    d. constant.
    Answer: B   Difficulty: I   Section: 4   Objective: 3

31. Spontaneous reactions are driven by
    a. decreasing enthalpy and decreasing entropy.
    b. decreasing enthalpy and increasing entropy.
    c. increasing enthalpy and decreasing entropy.
    d. increasing enthalpy and increasing entropy.
    Answer: B   Difficulty: I   Section: 4   Objective: 3

32. For a process in which ΔH is –298 kJ and ΔS is 100 J/K, calculate the change in the free energy at 0°C.
    a. -298 kJ
    b. -325 kJ
    c. -198 kJ
    d. -271kJ
    Answer: B   Difficulty: III   Section: 4   Objective: 3

COMPLETION

33. The energy released or absorbed during chemical change is called the ________.
    Answer: enthalpy of reaction
    Difficulty: I   Section: 1   Objective: 1

34. The unit of temperature in thermodynamic equations is the __________.
    Answer: kelvin   Difficulty: I   Section: 1   Objective: 2

35. The energy transferred between two objects that are at different temperatures is called __________.
    Answer: heat   Difficulty: I   Section: 1   Objective: 2

36. Molar heat capacity is expressed in units of _________.
    Answer: J/K·mol   Difficulty: I   Section: 1   Objective: 3

37. The term ________ refers to the amount of heat required to raise the temperature of 1 mole of a substance by 1 K.
    Answer: molar heat capacity
    Difficulty: I   Section: 1   Objective: 3

38. The terms c and C represent ________ and _______ in thermodynamic equations.
    Answer: specific heat and molar heat capacity
    Difficulty: I   Section: 1   Objective: 3

39. The science of _________ examines the energy changes in various processes.
    Answer: thermodynamics
    Difficulty: I   Section: 2   Objective: 1

40. The symbol ______ is used to indicate a change in enthalpy.
    Answer: ΔH Difficulty: I   Section: 2   Objective: 2

41. Adding energy to an object increases its ___________.
    Answer: enthalpy   Difficulty: I   Section: 2   Objective: 2

42. The molar heat capacity of most metals is about ___________.
    Answer: 25 J/K·mol Difficulty: I   Section: 2   Objective: 2

43. To calculate the energy released within a calorimeter, the _________, temperature change, and specific heat capacity of the water must be known.
    Answer: mass   Difficulty: I   Section: 3   Objective: 1

44. Instead of using a water bath, ___________ calorimetry measures the energy of the reactants in an insulating vessel.
    Answer: adiabatic   Difficulty: I   Section: 3   Objective: 1

45. According to ____________, the overall enthalpy change in a reaction is equal to the sum of the enthalpy changes of individual steps.
    Answer: Hess's law
    Difficulty: I   Section: 3   Objective: 2

46. The standard enthalpy of formation of a(n) __________ is equal to zero.
    Answer: element   Difficulty: I   Section: 3   Objective: 2

47. The term, ___________, describes the disorder in a system.
    Answer : entropy   Difficulty: I   Section: 4   Objective: 1

48. In the Gibb's energy equation, _____ is the symbol for entropy.
    Answer: S Difficulty: I   Section: 4   Objective: 1

49. As a solution becomes diluted, entropy ___________.
    Answer: increases   Difficulty: I   Section: 4   Objective: 1

50. The driving force of a reaction is the change in ________________.
    Answer: Gibbs energy
    Difficulty: I   Section: 4   Objective: 2

51. The symbol for the change in Gibbs energy is __________.
    Answer: ΔG Difficulty: I   Section: 4   Objective: 2

52. Entropy is expressed in units of __________.
    Answer: J/K   Difficulty: I   Section: 4   Objective: 2

53. A very large positive value of entropy tends to favor __________ of a chemical reaction.
    Answer : spontaneity
    Difficulty: I   Section: 4   Objective: 3

54. The quantity that predicts whether a reaction is spontaneous is _______________.
    Answer: Gibbs energy
    Difficulty: I   Section: 4   Objective: 3

55. Three factors, _______________, _______________, and _______________ affect the Gibbs energy of a reaction.
    Answer: enthalpy change, entropy change, and temperature
    Difficulty: I   Section: 4   Objective: 3

56. Chemical reactions are always spontaneous when ΔH is _____ and ΔS is _____.
    Answer: negative, positive
    Difficulty: I   Section: 4   Objective: 3

SHORT ANSWER

57. What is the enthalpy of a substance?

    Answer:

    The enthalpy is the total energy content of the material.

    Difficulty: I   Section: 1   Objective:

58. How can an iceberg (temperature = 0°C) have more energy than a burning match head (temperature = 230°C)?

    Answer:

    The iceberg has more energy because the iceberg is larger than the match.

    Difficulty: II   Section: 1   Objective: 2

59. Explain the difference between heat and temperature.

    Answer:

    Heat is energy that is transferred between objects. Temperature is a measure of the average kinetic energy of all the particles of a substance.

    Difficulty: II   Section: 1   Objective: 2

60. How is molar heat capacity related to specific heat?

    Answer:

    Specific heat is the amount of heat needed to raise the temperature of one gram of a material by 1 K. Molar heat capacity is the amount of heat needed to raise the temperature of one mole of the material by 1 K, so it is the specific heat multiplied by the molar mass.

    Difficulty: II   Section: 1   Objective: 3

61. What is thermodynamics?

    Answer:

    Thermodynamics is the science that studies the energy changes that accompany physical and chemical changes.

    Difficulty: I   Section: 2   Objective: 1

62. Why can ΔH be treated like other values in a stoichiometry problem even though it is not a physical product?

    Answer:

    ΔH is the energy that is released in a reaction, and it is proportional to the reactants. These proportions can be used as conversion factors in stoichiometry.

    Difficulty: II   Section: 2   Objective: 2

63. How can a calorimeter measure energy?

    Answer:

    When energy is released or absorbed inside the chamber of a calorimeter, the temperature of the water surrounding the chamber changes. The change in heat can be calculated by multiplying the mass of the water by the temperature change and by the specific heat of water.

    Difficulty: II   Section: 3   Objective: 1

64. If a calorimeter measures the temperature change of water, how is that value converted to heat?

    Answer:

    The temperature change of water can be converted to heat by multiplying the temperature change by the mass of the water and then multiplying this product by the specific heat capacity of water.

    Difficulty: II   Section: 3   Objective: 1

65. Explain the enthalpy change for a chemical reaction in terms of the enthalpies of its products and reactants.

    Answer:

    The enthalpy change for a reaction equals the total enthalpy of the products minus the total enthalpy of the reactants.

    Difficulty: II   Section: 3   Objective: 2

66. Explain why the effects of entropy increase as temperature increases.

    Answer:

    An increase in temperature causes particles to have more kinetic energy. This effect increases the movement of the particles, contributing to less order in the substance.

    Difficulty: II   Section: 4   Objective: 1

67. How does the Gibbs energy of a reaction relate to entropy and enthalpy?

    Answer:

    Gibbs energy is the quantity of energy remaining to do work after the energy associated with entropy has been subtracted from the enthalpy. To put this concept in mathematical terms, $\Delta G = \Delta H - T\Delta S$.

    Difficulty: II   Section: 4   Objective: 2

68. How is a change in Gibbs energy related to changes in enthalpy and entropy?

    Answer:

    The change in Gibbs energy is the difference between the change in enthalpy and the product of the Kelvin temperature and the entropy change. This relationship can be stated mathematically as $\Delta G = \Delta H - T\Delta S$.

    Difficulty: II   Section: 4   Objective: 2

69. How can an endothermic reaction like photosynthesis occur spontaneously?

    Answer:

    Generally, exothermic reactions are favored over endothermic reactions, but some endothermic reactions can occur if a sufficient source of energy is available to overcome the activation energy. Photosynthesis gains this energy from sunlight.

    Difficulty: II   Section: 4   Objective: 3

70. Describe how the driving forces of enthalpy or entropy determine the spontaneity of a chemical change.

    Answer:

    A spontaneous change generally involves a decrease in enthalpy. An increase in entropy often accompanies a spontaneous change. When only one of these conditions is true, spontaneity is determined by the equation $\Delta G = \Delta H - T\Delta S$.

    Difficulty: II   Section: 4   Objective: 3

71. How do the signs (+ or –) of ΔH and ΔS predict the spontaneity of a reaction?
    Answer:

    When both ΔH and ΔS are positive, the reaction is spontaneous only at high temperatures. When ΔH and ΔS are negative, the reaction is spontaneous only at low temperatures. The reaction is always spontaneous when ΔH is negative and ΔS is positive. The reaction is never spontaneous when ΔH is positive and ΔS is negative.
    Difficulty: II   Section: 4   Objective: 3

72. Describe when a chemical reaction will be spontaneous.
    Answer:

    A chemical reaction is spontaneous when the Gibbs energy, ΔG, is negative.
    Difficulty: II   Section: 4   Objective: 3

PROBLEMS

73. What is the molar change in enthalpy when 100 g of ice is heated from –18.2°C to –7.2°C? ($C = 37.4$ J/K·mol)
    Answer: $\Delta H = C \times \Delta T = (37.4\ \text{J/K·mol}) \times 11.0\ \text{K}$
    $\Delta H = 411.4\ \text{J/mol} = 0.411\ \text{kJ/mol}$
    Difficulty: III   Section: 2   Objective: 2

74. Use the information below to calculate the change in enthalpy for the reaction
    $H_2(g) + \frac{1}{2} O_2(g) \rightarrow H_2O(l)$

Reaction	ΔH
$H_2O(l) \rightarrow H_2O(g)$	44.0 kJ
$H_2O(l) \rightarrow H_2(g) + \frac{1}{2}\ O_2(g)$	241.8 kJ

    Answer: $H_2(g) + \frac{1}{2}\ O_2(g) \rightarrow H_2O(g)$ $\Delta H = -241.8$ kJ
                     $H_2O(g) \rightarrow H_2O(l)$ $\Delta H = -44.0$ kJ
    $\Delta H = -241.8$ kJ + (-44.0 kJ) = -285.8 kJ
    Difficulty: III   Section: 3   Objective: 3

75. Use the information below to determine ΔH for the reaction $Cu_2S(s) + S(s) \rightarrow 2CuS(s)$

Substance	ΔH°_f (kJ/mol)
Cu_2S	-79.5
S	0
CuS	-53.1

    Answer:
    $\Delta H = [\text{sum } \Delta H^0_f\ products] - [\text{sum } \Delta H^0_f\ reactants] = [2\ (-53.1)] - [-79.5 + 0] = -26.7$ kJ
    Difficulty: II   Section: 3   Objective: 3

76. Use the following data to determine the enthalpy of reaction for

$CuCl_2(s) + Cu(s) \rightarrow 2CuCl(s)$.

$CuCl_2(s) \rightarrow Cu(s) + Cl_2(g)$ $\Delta H = +206$ kJ

$2Cu(s) + Cl_2(g) \rightarrow 2CuCl(s)$ $\Delta H = -136$ kJ

Answer:
     ΔH = sum of steps = +206 + (–136) = +70.0 kJ

Difficulty: II   Section: 3   Objective: 3

77. Determine the entropy change for the following displacement reaction.

$Cl_2(g) + PbBr_2(aq) \rightarrow PbCl_2(aq) + Br_2(l)$.

Substance	ΔS (J/K mol)
$Cl_2(g)$	223.066
$PbBr_2(aq)$	182.7
$PbCl_2(aq)$	131.3
$Br_2(l)$	152.231

Answer:
     ΔS = [sum S products] – [sum S reactants] = [131.3 + 152.231] – [223.066 +182.7]
     = –122.2 J/K

Difficulty: II   Section: 4   Objective: 2

ESSAY QUESTIONS

78. How does temperature affect the Gibbs energy of a reaction?

Answer: The formula $\Delta G = \Delta H - T\Delta S$ shows that part of the energy change of a reaction is proportional to the temperature. Therefore, at higher temperatures, the contribution of the entropy change is more important in determining the Gibbs energy. At lower temperatures, the enthalpy change has more influence on the Gibbs energy.

Difficulty: II   Section: 4   Objective: 2

79. How does the Gibbs energy equation predict the progress of a chemical reaction?

Answer: The equation $\Delta G = \Delta H - T\Delta S$ shows that the Gibbs energy of a reaction depends on the enthalpy change, the entropy change, and the temperature of a reaction. If ΔG is negative, the change is spontaneous. If ΔG is positive, the change will not occur spontaneously. If ΔG is zero, neither the forward nor the reverse reaction is favored, so the result is a mixture of reactants and products.

Difficulty: II   Section: 4   Objective: 3

Solutions Manual

Solutions for problems can also be found at go.hrw.com. Enter the keyword HW4CHGTNS to obtain solutions.

Practice Problems A

1. Given: $C = 24.2$ J/K•mol $q = nC\Delta T$
    $\Delta T = 10.0$ K
    $n = 0.4$ mol $= (0.4 \text{ mol})(24.2 \text{ J/K•mol})(10.0 \text{ K})$

Unknown: q $= 97$ J

2. Given: $\Delta T = 2.5$ K $n = \dfrac{q}{C\Delta T}$
    $q = 1.7 \times 10^2$ J
    $C = 50.5$ J/K•mol $= \dfrac{1.7 \times 10^2 \text{ J}}{(50.5 \text{ J/K•mol})(2.5 \text{ K})}$

Unknown: n

                $= 1.3$ mol

3. Given: $n = 0.80$ mol $q = nC\Delta T$
    $\Delta T = 9.5$ K
    $C = 29.1$ J/K•mol $= (0.8 \text{ mol})(29.1 \text{ J/K•mol})(9.5 \text{ K})$

Unknown: q $= 220$ J

4. Given: $n = 0.07$ mol $\Delta T = \dfrac{q}{nC}$
    $q = 3.5 \times 10^3$ J
    $C = 254.0$ J/K•mol $= \dfrac{3.5 \times 10^3 \text{ J}}{(0.07 \text{ mol})(254.0 \text{ J/K•mol})}$

Unknown: ΔT

                $= 200$ K

Section 1 Review

8. Given: $q = 63$ J $n = \dfrac{m}{M}$
    $m = 1.2$ g
    $\Delta T = 1.0 \times 10^2$ K $= \dfrac{1.2 \text{ g}}{1.2 \text{ g/mol}}$

Unknown: C

                $= 0.1$ mol

            $C = \dfrac{q}{n\Delta T}$

                $= \dfrac{63 \text{ J}}{(0.1 \text{ mol})(1.0 \times 10^2 \text{ K})}$

                $= 6.3$ J/K•mol

Solutions Manual *continued*

9. Given: $C = 24.2$ J/K • mol $\Delta T = 125°C - 0°C$
   $m = 260.5$ g
   $T_i = 0°C$ $= 125°C = 125$ K
   $T_f = 125°C$

$$n = \frac{m}{M}$$

$$= \frac{260.5 \text{ g}}{26.98 \text{ g/mol}}$$

$$= 9.655 \text{ mol}$$

$$q = nC\Delta T$$

$$= (9.655 \text{ mol})(24.2 \text{ J/K} \bullet \text{mol})(125 \text{ K})$$

$$= 2.92 \times 10^4 \text{ J}$$

10. Given: $C = 25.1$ J/K • mol $\Delta T = 125°C - 0°C$
   $m = 260.5$ g
   $T_i = 0°C$ $= 125°C = 125$ K
   $T_f = 125°C$
   Unknown: q $n = \frac{m}{M}$

$$= \frac{260.5 \text{ g}}{55.85 \text{ g/mol}}$$

$$= 4.664 \text{ mol}$$

$$q = nC\Delta T$$

$$= (4.664 \text{ mol})(25.1 \text{ J/K} \bullet \text{mol})(125 \text{ K})$$

$$= 1.46 \times 10^4 \text{ J}$$

11. Given: $\Delta T = 3.5$ K $n = \dfrac{q}{C\Delta T}$
   $q = 1.67 \times 10^2$ J
   $C = 92.0$ J/K • mol
   Unknown: n $= \dfrac{1.67 \times 10^2 \text{ J}}{(92.0 \text{ J/K} \bullet \text{mol})(3.5 \text{ K})}$

$$= 0.52 \text{ mol}$$

12. Given: $C = 20.8$ J/K • mol $\Delta T = \dfrac{q}{nc}$
   $q = 2.5 \times 10^2$ J
   $n = 0.20$ mol
   $T_i = 298$ K $= \dfrac{2.5 \times 10^2 \text{ J}}{(0.20 \text{ mol})(20.8 \text{ J/K} \bullet \text{mol})}$
   Unknown: T_f

$$= 60 \text{ K}$$

$$T_f = \Delta T + T_i$$

$$= 60 \text{ K} + 298 \text{ K}$$

$$= 358 \text{ K}$$

Solutions Manual   Causes of Change

Solutions Manual *continued*

13. Given: $q = 1.2$ kJ
$V = 1.0 \times 10^2$ mL
$T_i = 298$ K
$C = 75.3$ J/K $\bullet$ mol

Unknown: T_f

$$n = 1.0 \times 10^2 \text{ mL} \times \frac{1.00 \text{ g}}{1.00 \text{ mL}} \times \frac{1.00 \text{ mol}}{18.0 \text{ g}}$$

$$= 5.6 \text{ mol}$$

$$\Delta T = \frac{q}{nc}$$

$$= \frac{1.2 \times 10^3 \text{ J}}{(5.6 \text{ mol})(75.3 \text{ J/K} \bullet \text{mol})}$$

$$= 2.8 \text{ K}$$

$$T_f = T_i - \Delta T$$

$$= 298 \text{ K} - 2.8 \text{ K}$$

$$= 295 \text{ K}$$

14. Given: $C = 25.3$ J/K $\bullet$ mol

Unknown: c

$$c = \frac{C}{M}$$

$$= \frac{25.3 \text{ J/K} \bullet \text{mol}}{107.87 \text{ g/mol}}$$

$$= 0.235 \text{ J/K} \bullet \text{g}$$

15. Given: $C = 50.5$ J/K $\bullet$ mol

Unknown: c

$$c = \frac{C}{M}$$

$$= \frac{50.5 \text{ J/K} \bullet \text{mol}}{58.44 \text{ g/mol}}$$

$$= 0.864 \text{ J/K} \bullet \text{g}$$

17. Given: PbS
Ag_2S

Unknown: C of PbS
C of Ag_2S

$$C_{PbS} = 2 \times 25 \text{ J/K} \bullet \text{mol}$$

$$= 50 \text{ J/K} \bullet \text{mol}$$

$$C_{Ag_2S} = 3 \times 25 \text{ J/K} \bullet \text{mol}$$

$$= 75 \text{ J/K} \bullet \text{mol}$$

18. Given: C of $AlCl_3 =$
92.0 J/K $\bullet$ mol

Unknown: C of $FeCl_3$

Each contains the same number of ions, so C of $FeCl_3$ would also be near 92.0 J/K $\bullet$ mol. Or 25 J/K mol $\times$ 4 = 100 J/K mol.

19. Given: C of $FeCl_3 =$
92.0 J/K $\bullet$ mol

Unknown: c

$$c = \frac{C}{M}$$

$$= \frac{92.0 \text{ J/K} \bullet \text{mol}}{162.20 \text{ g/mol}}$$

$$= 0.6 \text{ J/K} \bullet \text{g}$$

Solutions Manual *continued*

Practice Problems B

1. Given: $C = 75.3$ J/K • mol
$T_i = 41.7°C$
$T_f = 76.2°C$
Unknown: ΔH

$\Delta T = T_f - T_i$
$= 76.2°C - 41.7°C$
$= 34.5°C = 34.5$ K

$\Delta H = C\Delta T$
$= (75.3$ J/K • mol$)(34.5$ K$)$
$= 2.60$ kJ/mol

2. Given: $C = 50.5$ J/K • mol
$T_i = 0.0°C$
$T_f = 100.0°C$
Unknown: ΔH

$\Delta T = T_f - T_i$
$= 100.0°C - 0.0°C$
$= 100.0°C = 100.0$ K

$\Delta H = C\Delta T$
$= (50.5$ J/K • mol$)(100.0$ K$)$
$= 5.05$ kJ/mol

3. Given: $\Delta T = 15$ K
$C = 24.2$ J/K • mol
Unknown: ΔH

$\Delta H = C\Delta T$
$= (24.2$ J/K • mol$)(15$ K$)$
$= 360$ J/mol

Practice Problems C

1. Given: $C = 24.2$ J/K • mol
$T_i = 128.5°C$
$T_f = 22.6°C$
Unknown: ΔH

$\Delta T = T_f - T_i$
$= 22.6°C - 128.5°C$
$= -105.9°C = -105.9$ K

$\Delta H = C\Delta T$
$= (24.2$ J/K • mol$)(-105.9$ K$)$
$= -2.56$ kJ/mol

2. Given: $C = 26.4$ J/K • mol
$T_i = 302°C$
$T_f = 275°C$
Unknown: ΔH

$\Delta T = T_f - T_i$
$= 275°C - 302°C$
$= -27°C = -27$ K

$\Delta H = C\Delta T$
$= (26.4$ J/K • mol$)(-27$ K$)$
$= -713$ J/mol

Solutions Manual *continued*

3. Given: $C = 27.8$ J/K $\bullet$ mol $\Delta H = C\Delta T$
      $\Delta T = -10$ K
     Unknown: ΔH
$$= (27.8 \text{ J/K} \bullet \text{mol})(-10 \text{ K})$$
$$= -280 \text{ J/mol}$$

Section 2 Review

4. Given: $T_i = -0.5°C$ $\Delta T = T_f - T_i$
       $T_f = -10.1°C$
    Unknown: ΔT in °C and
           K
$$= -10.1°C - (-0.5°C)$$
$$= -9.6°C = -9.6 \text{ K}$$

5. Given: $C = 37.4$ J/K $\bullet$ mol $\Delta T = T_f - T_i$
      $T_i = -8.4°C$
      $T_f = -5.2°C$
    Unknown: ΔH
$$= -5.2°C - (-8.4°C)$$
$$= 3.2°C = 3.2 \text{ K}$$
$$\Delta H = C\Delta T$$
$$= (37.4 \text{ J/K} \bullet \text{mol})(3.2 \text{ K})$$
$$= 1.2 \times 10^2 \text{ J/mol}$$

6. Given: $C = 75.3$ J/K $\bullet$ mol $\Delta T = T_f - T_i$
      $T_i = 48.3°C$
      $T_f = 25.2°C$
    Unknown: ΔH
$$= 25.2°C - 48.3°C$$
$$= -23.1°C = -23.1 \text{ K}$$
$$\Delta H = C\Delta T$$
$$= (75.3 \text{ J/K} \bullet \text{mol})(-23.1 \text{ K})$$
$$= -1.74 \text{ kJ/mol}$$

7. Given: $C = 136$ J/K $\bullet$ mol $\Delta T = T_f - T_i$
      $T_i = 19.7°C$
      $T_f = 46.8°C$
    Unknown: ΔH
$$= 46.8°C - 19.7°C$$
$$= 27.1°C = 27.1 \text{ K}$$
$$\Delta H = C\Delta T$$
$$= (136 \text{ J/K} \bullet \text{mol})(27.1 \text{ K})$$
$$= 3.69 \text{ kJ/mol}$$

8. Given: $C = 172$ J/K $\bullet$ mol $\Delta T = \dfrac{\Delta H}{C}$
      $\Delta H = -186.9$ J/mol
    Unknown: ΔT
$$= \frac{-186.9 \text{ J/mol}}{172 \text{ J/K} \bullet \text{mol}}$$
$$= -1.09 \text{ K}$$

9. Given: $\Delta H = -428$ J/mol $C = \dfrac{\Delta H}{\Delta T}$
       $\Delta T = -10.0$ K
    Unknown: C
$$= \frac{-428 \text{ J/mol}}{-10.0 \text{ K}}$$
$$= 42.8 \text{ J/K} \bullet \text{mol}$$

Solutions Manual *continued*

11. Given: $\Delta T = 40$ K
$\quad\quad C = 25$ J/K $\cdot$ mol
$\quad$ Unknown: ΔH

$\Delta H = C\Delta T$

$\quad = (25$ J/K $\cdot$ mol$)(40$ K$)$

$\quad = 1.0 \times 10^3$ J/mol

Practice Problems D

1. Given: $NO(g) + \frac{1}{2}O_2(g) \rightarrow$
$\quad\quad\quad NO_2(g)$
$\quad \Delta H^0_{f\,NO} =$
$\quad\quad\quad 91$ kJ/mol
$\quad \Delta H^0_{f\,NO_2} =$
$\quad\quad\quad 33$ kJ/mol
$\quad$ Unknown: ΔH

$NO(g) \rightarrow \frac{1}{2}N_2(g) + \frac{1}{2}O_2(g)$ $\quad\quad\quad\quad \Delta H = -90.3$ kJ/mol

$\frac{1}{2}N_2(g) + O_2(g) \rightarrow NO_2(g)$ $\quad\quad\quad\quad \Delta H = 33.1$ kJ/mol

$NO(g) + \frac{1}{2}\cancel{N_2(g)} + O_2(g) \rightarrow \frac{1}{2}\cancel{N_2(g)} + \frac{1}{2}O_2(g) + NO_2(g)$

$\Delta H = -90.3$ kJ/mol $+ 33.1$ kJ/mol

$NO(g) + \frac{1}{2}O_2(g) \rightarrow NO_2(g)$

$\Delta H = -57.2$ kJ/mol

2. Given: $\Delta H^0_f\,C_0H_4 =$
$\quad\quad\quad -74.81$ kJ/mol
$\quad \Delta H^0_f\,C_{O_2} =$
$\quad\quad\quad -393.509$ kJ/mol
$\quad \Delta H^0_f\,H_2O(l) =$
$\quad\quad\quad -285.830$ kJ/mol
$\quad$ Unknown: ΔH for
$\quad\quad\quad$ combustion
$\quad\quad\quad$ of $CH_4(g)$

$CH_4(g) + 2O_2(g) \rightarrow CO_2(g) + 2H_2O(l)$

$\quad C(s) + O_2(g) \rightarrow CO_2(g)$ $\quad\quad\quad\quad \Delta H^0_f = -393.5$ kJ/mol

$\quad 2(H_2(g) + \frac{1}{2}O_2(g) \rightarrow H_2O(l)$ $\quad\quad\quad \Delta H^0_f = -285.8$ kJ/mol$)$

$\quad CH_4(g) \rightarrow C(s) + 2H_2(g)$ $\quad\quad\quad\quad \Delta H^0_f = 74.9$ kJ/mol

$\quad C(s) + O_2(g) \rightarrow CO_2(g)$ $\quad\quad\quad\quad \Delta H^0_f = -393.5$ kJ/mol

$\quad 2H_2(g) + O_2(g) \rightarrow 2H_2O(l)$ $\quad\quad\quad \Delta H^0_f = -571.6$ kJ/mol

$\quad CH_4(g) \rightarrow C(s) + 2H_2(g)$ $\quad\quad\quad\quad \Delta H^0_f = 74.9$ kJ/mol

$CH_4(g) + 2O_2(g) \rightarrow CO_2(g) + 2H_2O(l)$ $\quad \Delta H^0_f = -890.2$ kJ/mol

Practice Problems E

1. Given:
$\quad C_2H_6(g) + \frac{7}{2}O_2(g) \rightarrow$
$\quad\quad 2CO_2(g) + 3H_2O(g)$
$\quad$ for $C_2H_6(g)$,
$\quad\quad \Delta H^0_f = -83.8$ kJ/mol
$\quad$ for $O_2(g)$,
$\quad\quad\quad \Delta H^0_f = 0$ kJ/mol
$\quad$ for $CO_2(g)$,
$\quad\quad \Delta H^0_f = -393.5$ kJ/mol
$\quad$ for $H_2O(g)$,
$\quad\quad \Delta H^0_f = -241.8$ kJ/mol
$\quad$ Unknown: ΔH for the
$\quad\quad\quad$ reaction

$\Delta H = \Delta H^0_f(\text{products}) - \Delta H^0_f(\text{reactants})$

$\quad = 2$ mol$(-393.5$ kJ/mol$) + 3$ mol$(-241.8$ kJ/mol$) -$
$\quad\quad 1$ mol$(-83.8$ kJ/mol$) - \frac{7}{2}$ mol$(0$ kJ/mol$)$

$\quad = -787$ kJ $- 725.4$ kJ $+ 83.8$ kJ $+ 0$ kJ

$\quad = -1428.6$ kJ

Solutions Manual *continued*

2. Given:

$CaO(s) + H_2O(l) \rightarrow Ca(OH)_2(s)$

for $CaO(s)$,
$\Delta H_f^0 = -634.9$ kJ/mol

for $H_2O(l)$,
$\Delta H_f^0 = -285.8$ kJ/mol

for $Ca(OH)_2(s)$,
$\Delta H_f^0 = -985.2$ kJ/mol

Unknown: ΔH for the reaction

$\Delta H = \Delta H_f^0(\text{products}) - \Delta H_f^0(\text{reactants})$

$= 1 \text{ mol}(-985.2 \text{ kJ/mol}) - 1 \text{ mol}(-634.9 \text{ kJ/mol}) - 1 \text{ mol}(-285.8 \text{ kJ/mol})$

$= -64.5$ kJ

Section 3 Review

4. Given:

for $CaCO_3(s)$,
$\Delta H_f^0 = -1206.9$ kJ/mol

for $CaO(s)$,
$\Delta H_f^0 = -634.9$ kJ/mol

for $CO_2(g)$,
$\Delta H_f^0 = -393.5$ kJ/mol

Unknown: ΔH for the reaction

$CaCO_3(s) \rightarrow CaO(s) + CO_2(g)$

$\Delta H = \Delta H_f^0(\text{products}) - \Delta H_f^0(\text{reactants})$

$= 1 \text{ mol}(-634.9 \text{ kJ/mol}) + 1 \text{ mol}(-393.5 \text{ kJ/mol}) - 1 \text{ mol}(-1206.9 \text{ kJ/mol})$

$= 178.5$ kJ

5. Given:

$2Al(s) + 3H_2O(l) \rightarrow Al_2O_3(s) + 3H_2(g)$

for $Al(s)$, $\Delta H_f^0 = 0$ kJ/mol

for $H_2O(l)$,
$\Delta H_f^0 = -285.8$ kJ/mol

for $Al_2O_3(s)$,
$\Delta H_f^0 = -1676.0$ kJ/mol

for $H_2(g)$, $\Delta H_f^0 = 0$ kJ/mol

Unknown: ΔH for the reaction

$\Delta H = \Delta H_f^0(\text{products}) - \Delta H_f^0(\text{reactants})$

$= 1 \text{ mol}(-1676.0 \text{ kJ/mol}) + 3 \text{ mol}(0 \text{ kJ/mol}) - 2 \text{ mol}(0 \text{ kJ/mol}) - 3 \text{ mol}(-285.8 \text{ kJ/mol})$

$= -818.6$ kJ

Practice Problems F

1. Given:

$CO(g) + 2H_2(g) \rightarrow CH_3OH(l)$

for $CO(g)$,
$S^0 = 197.6$ J/K $\bullet$ mol

for $H_2(g)$,
$S^0 = 130.7$ J/K $\bullet$ mol

for $CH_3OH(l)$,
$S^0 = 126.8$ J/K $\bullet$ mol

Unknown: ΔS

$\Delta S = \Delta S^0(\text{products}) - \Delta S^0(\text{reactants})$

$= 1 \text{ mol}(126.8 \text{ J/K} \bullet \text{mol}) - 1 \text{ mol}(197.6 \text{ J/K} \bullet \text{mol}) - 2 \text{ mol}(130.7 \text{ J/K} \bullet \text{mol})$

$= -332.2$ J/K

Solutions Manual *continued*

2. Given:
$$\tfrac{1}{2}CO(g) + H_2(g) \rightarrow \tfrac{1}{2}CH_3OH(l)$$
for $CO(g)$,
$$S^0 = 197.6 \text{ J/K} \bullet \text{mol}$$
for $H_2(g)$,
$$S^0 = 130.7 \text{ J/K} \bullet \text{mol}$$
for $CH_3OH(l)$,
$$S^0 = 126.8 \text{ J/K} \bullet \text{mol}$$
Unknown: ΔS

$\Delta S = \Delta S^0(\text{products}) - \Delta S^0(\text{reactants})$

$= \tfrac{1}{2} \text{ mol}(126.8 \text{ J/K} \bullet \text{mol}) - \tfrac{1}{2} \text{ mol}(197.6 \text{ J/K} \bullet \text{mol}) -$
$1 \text{ mol}(130.7 \text{ J/K} \bullet \text{mol})$

$= -166.1 \text{ J/K}$

3. Given:
$$2Na(s) + Cl_2(g) \rightarrow 2Na^+(aq) + 2Cl^-(aq)$$
for $NaCl(s) \rightarrow Na^+(aq) + Cl^-(aq)$,
$$\Delta S = 43 \text{ J/K}$$
for $2Na(s) + Cl_2(g) \rightarrow 2NaCl(s)$,
$$\Delta S = -181 \text{ J/K}$$
Unknown: ΔS

$2NaCl(s) \rightarrow 2Na^+(aq) + 2Cl^-(aq)$	$\Delta S = 2(43 \text{ J/K})$
$2Na(s) + Cl_2(g) \rightarrow 2NaCl(s)$	$\Delta S = -181 \text{ J/K}$
$2Na(s) + Cl_2(g) \rightarrow 2Na^+(aq) + 2Cl^-(aq)$	$\Delta S = -95 \text{ J/K}$

Practice Problems G

1. Given: $\Delta H = -76 \text{ kJ}$
$\Delta S = -117 \text{ J/K}$
$= -0.117 \text{ kJ/K}$
$T = 298.15 \text{ K}$
Unknown: spontaneous or not

$\Delta G = \Delta H - T\Delta S$

$= -76 \text{ kJ} - (298.15 \text{ K})(-0.117 \text{ kJ/K})$

$= -41 \text{ kJ}$

ΔG is negative, so the reaction is spontaneous.

2. Given: $\Delta H = 11 \text{ kJ}$
$\Delta S = 49 \text{ J/K}$
$= 0.049 \text{ kJ/K}$
$T = 298.15 \text{ K}$
Unknown: ΔG, spontaneous or not

$\Delta G = \Delta H - T\Delta S$

$= 11 \text{ kJ} - (298.15 \text{ K})(0.049 \text{ kJ/K})$

$= -3.6 \text{ kJ}$

ΔG is negative, so the reaction is spontaneous.

3. Given: $\Delta H = 11 \text{ kJ}$
$\Delta S = 41 \text{ J/K}$
$= 0.041 \text{ kJ/K}$
$T = 298.15 \text{ K}$
Unknown: spontaneous or not, ΔG

$\Delta G = \Delta H - T\Delta S$

$= 11 \text{ kJ} - (298.15 \text{ K})(0.041 \text{ kJ/K})$

$= -1.2 \text{ kJ}$

ΔG is negative, so the reaction is spontaneous.

Practice Problems H

1. Given: $C(s) + O_2(g) \rightarrow CO_2(g)$
for $C(s)$, $\Delta G_f^0 = 0 \text{ kJ/mol}$
for $O_2(g)$, $\Delta G_f^0 = 0 \text{ kJ/mol}$
for $CO_2(g)$,
$\Delta G_f^0 = -393.4 \text{ kJ/mol}$
Unknown: ΔG, spontaneous or not

$\Delta G = \Delta G_f^0(\text{products}) - \Delta G_f^0(\text{reactants})$

$= 1 \text{ mol}(-394.4 \text{ kJ/mol}) - 1 \text{ mol}(0 \text{ kJ/mol}) - 1 \text{ mol}(0 \text{ kJ/mol})$

$= -394.4 \text{ kJ}$

ΔG is negative, so the reaction is spontaneous.

Solutions Manual *continued*

2. Given: $CaCO_3(s) \rightarrow$
$\qquad\qquad CaO(s) + CO_2(g)$
for $CaCO_3(s)$,
$\qquad \Delta G_f^0 = -1128.8 \text{ kJ/mol}$
for $CaO(s)$,
$\qquad \Delta G_f^0 = -604.0 \text{ kJ/mol}$
for $CO_2(g)$,
$\qquad \Delta G_f^0 = -394.4 \text{ kJ/mol}$

Unknown: ΔG, sponta-
$\qquad$ neous or not

$\Delta G = \Delta G_f^0(\text{products}) - \Delta G_f^0(\text{reactants})$

$\qquad = 1 \text{ mol}(-604.0 \text{ kJ/mol}) + 1 \text{ mol}(-394.4 \text{ kJ/mol}) -$
$\qquad\quad 1 \text{ mol}(-1128.8 \text{ kJ/mol})$

$\qquad = 130.4 \text{ kJ/mol}$

ΔG is positive, so the reaction is not spontaneous.

Section 4 Review

7. Given:
for $NO(g)$,
$\qquad S^0 = 210.8 \text{ J/K} \cdot \text{mol}$
for $NO_2(g)$,
$\qquad S^0 = 240.1 \text{ J/K} \cdot \text{mol}$
for $O_2(g)$,
$\qquad S^0 = 205.1 \text{ J/K} \cdot \text{mol}$
$2NO(g) + O_2(g) \rightarrow$
$\qquad\qquad 2NO_2(g)$

Unknown: ΔS

$\Delta S = \Delta S^0(\text{products}) - \Delta S^0(\text{reactants})$

$\qquad = 2 \text{ mol}(240.1 \text{ J/K} \cdot \text{mol}) - 2 \text{ mol}(210.8 \text{ J/K} \cdot \text{mol}) -$
$\qquad\quad 1 \text{ mol}(205.1 \text{ J/K} \cdot \text{mol})$

$\qquad = -146.5 \text{ J/K}$

8. Given: $X(s) + 2Y_2(g) \rightarrow$
$\qquad\qquad XY_4(g)$
$\qquad \Delta H = -74.8 \text{ kJ}$
$\qquad \Delta S = -80.8 \text{ J/K}$
$\qquad\quad = -0.0808 \text{ kJ/K}$

Unknown: ΔG

$\Delta G = \Delta H - T\Delta S$

$\qquad = -74.8 \text{ kJ} - (298.15 \text{ K})(-0.0808 \text{ kJ/K})$

$\qquad = -50.7 \text{ kJ}$

9. Given:
$CaCl_2(s) + H_2O(g) \rightarrow$
$\qquad\qquad CaO(s) + 2HCl(g)$
for $CaCl_2(s)$,
$\qquad \Delta G_f^0 = -748.1 \text{ kJ/mol}$
for $H_2O(g)$,
$\qquad \Delta G_f^0 = -228.6 \text{ kJ/mol}$
for $CaO(s)$,
$\qquad \Delta G_f^0 = -604.0 \text{ kJ/mol}$
for $HCl(g)$,
$\qquad \Delta G_f^0 = -95.3 \text{ kJ/mol}$

Unknown: whether the
$\qquad$ reaction is
$\qquad$ spontaneous
$\qquad$ or not

$\Delta G = \Delta G_f^0(\text{products}) - \Delta G_f^0(\text{reactants})$

$\qquad = 1 \text{ mol}(-604.0 \text{ kJ/mol}) + 2 \text{ mol}(-95.3 \text{ kJ/mol}) -$
$\qquad\quad 1 \text{ mol}(-748.1 \text{ kJ/mol}) - 1 \text{ mol}(-228.6 \text{ kJ/mol})$

$\qquad = 182. \text{ kJ}$

The reaction is not spontaneous because ΔG is positive.

10. Given:
$2CO(g) \rightarrow C(s) + CO_2(g)$
for $CO(g)$,
$\qquad \Delta G_f^0 = -137.2 \text{ kJ/mol}$
for $C(s)$, $\Delta G_f^0 = 0 \text{ kJ/mol}$
for $CO_2(g)$,
$\qquad \Delta G_f^0 = -394.4 \text{ kJ/mol}$

Unknown: ΔG

$\Delta G = \Delta G_f^0(\text{products}) - \Delta G_f^0(\text{reactants})$

$\qquad = 1 \text{ mol}(0 \text{ kJ/mol}) + 1 \text{ mol}(-394.4 \text{ kJ/mol}) - 2 \text{ mol}(-137.2 \text{ kJ/mol})$

$\qquad = -120.0 \text{ kJ}$

Solutions Manual *continued*

12. Given: spontaneous reaction
$\Delta H = 8$ kJ
$T = 25°C$
$= 298$ K

Unknown: ΔS to give a negative ΔG

$\Delta G = \Delta H - T\Delta S$

$0 > 8$ kJ $- 298$ K(ΔS)

8 kJ < 298 K(ΔS)

$\Delta S > 0.03$ kJ/K

---

13. Given: balanced chemical equations
for HCl(g),
$\Delta G_f^0 = -95.3$ kJ/mol
for CHCl$_3$(l),
$\Delta G_f^0 = -73.66$ kJ/mol
for C(s), H$_2$(g), and Cl$_2$(g),
$\Delta G_f^0 = 0$ kJ/mol
for CH$_4$(g),
$\Delta G_f^0 = -50.7$ kJ/mol
for CO(g),
$\Delta G_f^0 = -137.2$ kJ/mol
for H$_2$O(l),
$\Delta G_f^0 = -237.2$ kJ/mol

Unknown: which reactions are effective

$\Delta G = \Delta G_f^0(\text{products}) - \Delta G_f^0(\text{reactants})$

for $2C(s) + H_2(g) + 3Cl_2(g) \rightarrow 2CHCl_3(l)$:

$\Delta G = 2$ mol$(-73.66$ kJ/mol$) - 6$ mol$(0$ kJ/mol$)$

$\quad = -147.3$ kJ

for $C(s) + HCl(g) + Cl_2(g) \rightarrow CHCl_3(l)$:

$\Delta G = 1$ mol$(-73.66$ kJ/mol$) - 2$ mol$(0$ kJ/mol$) -$
$\quad 1$ mol$(-95.3$ kJ/mol$)$

$\quad = 21.6$ kJ

for $CH_4(g) + 3Cl_2(g) \rightarrow CHCl_3(l) + 3HCl(g)$:

$\Delta G = 1$ mol$(-73.66$ kJ/mol$) + 3$ mol$(-95.3$ kJ/mol$) -$
$\quad 1$ mol$(-50.7$ kJ/mol$) - 3$ mol$(0$ kJ/mol$)$

$\quad = -308.9$ kJ

for $CO(g) + 3HCl(g) \rightarrow CHCl_3(l) + H_2O(l)$:

$\Delta G = 1$ mol$(-73.66$ kJ/mol$) + 1$ mol$(-237.2$ kJ/mol$) -$
$\quad 1$ mol$(-137.2$ kJ/mol$) - 3$ mol$(-95.3$ kJ/mol$)$

$\quad = 112.5$ kJ/mol

The first and third reactions have highly negative ΔGs, so they will be quite spontaneous and should be investigated.

Chapter Review

27. Given: $q = 70.2$ J
$T_i = 23.0°C$
$T_f = 24.0°C$
$m = 34.0$ g

Unknown: C

$\Delta T = T_f - T_i$

$\quad = 24.0°C - 23.0°C$

$\quad = 1.0°C = 1.0$ K

$n = \dfrac{m}{M}$

$\quad = \dfrac{34.0 \text{ g}}{17.04 \text{ g/mol}}$

$\quad = 2.00$ mol

$C = \dfrac{q}{n\Delta T}$

$\quad = \dfrac{70.2 \text{ J}}{(2.00 \text{ mol})(1.0 \text{ K})}$

$\quad = 35.2$ J/K $\bullet$ mol

Solutions Manual *continued*

28. Given: $n = 1.0$ mol
$q = 53$ J
In $(S, 297.5$ K$) \rightarrow$
  In $(S, 299.5$ K$)$
Unknown: C

$\Delta T = T_f - T_i$

$= 299.5$ K $- 297.5$ K

$= 2.0$ K

$C = \dfrac{q}{n \Delta T}$

$= \dfrac{53 \text{ J}}{(1.0 \text{ mol})(2.0 \text{ K})}$

$= 27$ J/K $\bullet$ mol

29. Given: $T_i = 233$ K
$T_f = 475$ K
$C = 29.1$ J/K $\bullet$ mol
Unknown: ΔH

$\Delta T = T_f - T_i$

$= 475$ K $- 233$ K

$= 242$ K

$\Delta H = C \Delta T$

$= (29.1 \text{ J/K} \bullet \text{mol})(242 \text{ K})$

$= 7.04$ kJ/mol

30. Given: $\Delta T = 15°C = 15$K
$C = 27.8$ J/K $\bullet$ mol
Unknown: ΔH

$\Delta H = C \Delta T$

$= (27.8 \text{ J/K} \bullet \text{mol})(15 \text{ K})$

$= 4.2 \times 10^2$ J/mol $\times 0.055$ mol $= 23$ J

31. Given: $C = 20.8$ J/K $\bullet$ mol
$T_i = 475$ K
$T_f = 233$ K
Unknown: ΔH

$\Delta T = T_f - T_i$

$= 233$ K $- 475$ K

$= -242$ K

$\Delta H = C \Delta T$

$= (20.8 \text{ J/K} \bullet \text{mol})(-242 \text{ K})$

$= -5.03$ kJ/mol

32. Given: $C = 75.1$ J/K $\bullet$ mol
$T_i = 15°C$
$T_f = -30°C$
Unknown: ΔH

$\Delta T = T_f - T_i$

$= -30°C - 15°C$

$= -45°C = -45$ K

$\Delta H = C \Delta T$

$= (75.1 \text{ J/K} \bullet \text{mol})(-45 \text{ K})(0.54 \text{ mol})$

$= 1800$ J

Solutions Manual *continued*

33. Given: balanced chemical equations for steps and overall reaction energy diagram

Unknown: ΔH for each step and the net reaction

$$Sn(s) + Cl_2(g) \rightarrow SnCl_2(l) \qquad \Delta H = -325.1 \text{ kJ}$$
$$SnCl_2(s) + Cl_2(g) \rightarrow SnCl_4(l) \qquad \Delta H = -186.2 \text{ kJ}$$
$$\overline{Sn(s) + 2Cl_2(g) \rightarrow SnCl_4(l) \qquad \Delta H = -511.3 \text{ kJ}}$$

34. Given:
$$4Al(s) + 6H_2O(l) \rightarrow 2Al_2O_3(s) + 6H_2(g)$$
for $Al(s)$ and $H_2(g)$,
$$\Delta H_f^0 = 0 \text{ kJ/mol}$$
for $H_2O(l)$,
$$\Delta H_f^0 = -285.8 \text{ kJ/mol}$$
for $Al_2O_3(s)$,
$$\Delta H_f^0 = -1676.0 \text{ kJ/mol}$$

Unknown: ΔH for the reaction, exothermic or not

$$\Delta H = \Delta H_f^0(\text{products}) - \Delta H_f^0(\text{reactants})$$
$$= 2 \text{ mol}(-1676.0 \text{ kJ/mol}) + 6 \text{ mol}(0 \text{ kJ/mol}) -$$
$$4 \text{ mol}(0 \text{ kJ/mol}) - 6 \text{ mol}(-285.8 \text{ kJ/mol})$$
$$= -1637 \text{ kJ}$$

The reaction is exothermic.

35. Given:
$$2Fe_2O_3(s) + 3C(s) \rightarrow 4Fe(s) + 3CO_2(g)$$
for $Fe_2O_3(s)$,
$$\Delta H_f^0 = -824.2 \text{ kJ/mol}$$
for $C(s)$ and $Fe(s)$,
$$\Delta H_f^0 = 0 \text{ kJ/mol}$$
for $CO_2(g)$,
$$\Delta H_f^0 = -393.5 \text{ kJ/mol}$$

Unknown: ΔH per 1 mol of Fe

$$\tfrac{1}{2}Fe_2O_3(s) + \tfrac{3}{4}C(s) \rightarrow Fe(s) + \tfrac{3}{4}CO_2(g)$$
$$\Delta H = \Delta H_f^0(\text{products}) - \Delta H_f^0(\text{reactants})$$
$$= 1 \text{ mol}(0 \text{ kJ/mol}) + \tfrac{3}{4} \text{ mol}(-393.5 \text{ kJ/mol}) -$$
$$\tfrac{1}{2} \text{ mol}(-824.2 \text{ kJ/mol}) - \tfrac{3}{4} \text{ mol}(0 \text{ kJ/mol})$$
$$= 117.6 \text{ kJ}$$

36. Given:
for $C_6H_{12}O_6(s)$,
$$\Delta H_f^0 = -1263 \text{ kJ/mol}$$
for $CO_2(g)$,
$$\Delta H_f^0 = -393.5 \text{ kJ/mol}$$
for $H_2O(l)$,
$$\Delta H_f^0 = -285.8 \text{ kJ/mol}$$
for $O_2(g)$, $\Delta H_f^0 = 0 \text{ kJ/mol}$

Unknown: ΔH

$$C_6H_{12}O_6(s) + 6O_2(g) \rightarrow 6CO_2(g) + 6 H_2O(l)$$
$$\Delta H = \Delta H_f^0(\text{products}) - \Delta H_f^0(\text{reactants})$$
$$= 6 \text{ mol}(-393.5 \text{ kJ/mol}) + 6 \text{ mol}(-285.8 \text{ kJ/mol}) -$$
$$1 \text{ mol}(-1263 \text{ kJ/mol}) - 6 \text{ mol}(0 \text{ kJ/mol})$$
$$= -2813 \text{ kJ}$$

37. Given:
for $S_8(s) + 8O_2(g) \rightarrow 8SO_2(g)$, $\Delta S = 89 \text{ J/K}$
for $2SO_2(g) + O_2(g) \rightarrow 2SO_3(g)$, $\Delta S = -188 \text{ J/K}$
$$S_8(s) + 12O_2(g) \rightarrow 8SO_3(g)$$

Unknown: ΔS

$$4[2SO_2(g) + O_2(g) \rightarrow 2SO_3(g), \Delta S = -188 \text{ J/K}] =$$
$$8SO_2(g) + 4O_2(g) \rightarrow 8SO_3(g), \Delta S = -752 \text{ J/K}$$

$$S_8(s) + 8O_2(g) \rightarrow 8SO_2(g), \Delta S = 89 \text{ J/K}$$

$$8SO_2(g) + 4O_2(g) \rightarrow 8SO_3(g), \Delta S = -752 \text{ J/K}$$

$$S_8(s) + \cancel{8SO_2(g)} + 12O_2(g) \rightarrow \cancel{8SO_2(g)} + 8SO_3(g), \Delta S = -663 \text{ J/K}$$

Solutions Manual *continued*

38. Given:
for $MgO(s)$,
$$\Delta S = 26.9 \text{ J/K} \cdot \text{mol}$$
for $CO_2(g)$,
$$\Delta S = 213.7 \text{ J/K} \cdot \text{mol}$$
for $MgCO_3(s)$,
$$\Delta S = 65.7 \text{ J/K} \cdot \text{mol}$$
$$MgCO_3(s) \rightarrow$$
$$MgO(s) + CO_2(g)$$
Unknown: ΔS

$$\Delta S = \Delta S(\text{products}) - \Delta S(\text{reactants})$$
$$= 1 \text{ mol}(26.9 \text{ J/K} \cdot \text{mol}) + 1 \text{ mol}(213.7 \text{ J/K} \cdot \text{mol}) -$$
$$1 \text{ mol}(65.7 \text{ J/K} \cdot \text{mol})$$
$$= 174.9 \text{ J/K}$$

39. Given: $\Delta H = -356 \text{ kJ}$
$$\Delta S = -36 \text{ J/K}$$
$$T = 25°C$$
$$= 298 \text{ K}$$
Unknown: ΔG, spontaneous or not

$$\Delta G = \Delta H - T\Delta S$$
$$= -356 \text{ kJ} - (298 \text{ K})(-0.036 \text{ kJ/K})$$
$$= -345 \text{ kJ}$$
ΔG is negative, so the reaction is spontaneous.

40. Given: $\Delta H = 98 \text{ kJ}$
$$\Delta S = 292 \text{ J/K}$$
$$T = 25°C$$
$$= 298 \text{ K}$$
Unknown: spontaneous or not effect of increased temperature

$$\Delta G = \Delta H - T\Delta S$$
$$= 98 \text{ kJ} - (298 \text{ K})(0.292 \text{ kJ/K})$$
$$= 11 \text{ kJ}$$
ΔG is positive, so the reaction is not spontaneous. If T is increased to 336 K, the reaction will be spontaneous.

41. Given:
$$4CO(g) + 2H_2O(g) \rightarrow$$
$$CH_4(g) + 3CO_2(g)$$
for $CO(g)$,
$$\Delta G_f^0 = -137.2 \text{ kJ/mol}$$
for $H_2O(g)$,
$$\Delta G_f^0 = -228.6 \text{ kJ/mol}$$
for $CH_4(g)$,
$$\Delta G_f^0 = -50.7 \text{ kJ/mol}$$
for $CO_2(g)$,
$$\Delta G_f^0 = -394.4 \text{ kJ/mol}$$
Unknown: ΔG, spontaneous or not

$$\Delta G = \Delta G_f^0(\text{products}) - \Delta G_f^0(\text{reactants})$$
$$= 1 \text{ mol}(-50.7 \text{ kJ/mol}) + 3 \text{ mol}(-394.4 \text{ kJ/mol}) -$$
$$4 \text{ mol}(-137.2 \text{ kJ/mol}) - 2 \text{ mol}(-228.6 \text{ kJ/mol})$$
$$= -227.9 \text{ kJ}$$
ΔG is negative, so the reaction is spontaneous.

42. Given:
$$C_{12}H_{22}O_{11}(aq) + H_2O(l) \rightarrow$$
$$2C_6H_{12}O_6(aq)$$
for $C_6H_{12}O_6(aq)$,
$$\Delta G_f^0 = -915 \text{ kJ/mol}$$
for $C_{12}H_{22}O_{11}(aq)$,
$$\Delta G_f^0 = -1551 \text{ kJ/mol}$$
for $H_2O(l)$,
$$\Delta G_f^0 = -237.2 \text{ kJ/mol}$$
Unknown: spontaneous or not

$$\Delta G = \Delta G_f^0(\text{products}) - \Delta G_f^0(\text{reactants})$$
$$= 2 \text{ mol}(-915 \text{ kJ/mol}) - 1 \text{ mol}(-1551 \text{ kJ/mol}) -$$
$$1 \text{ mol}(-237.2 \text{ kJ/mol})$$
$$= -42 \text{ kJ}$$
ΔG is negative, so the reaction is likely to occur.

Solutions Manual *continued*

44. Given:
$$CH_2O(g) + CO_2(g) \rightarrow$$
$$H_2O(g) + 2CO(g)$$
for $CH_2O(g)$,
$$\Delta H_f^0 = -109 \text{ kJ/mol}$$
for $CO_2(g)$,
$$\Delta H_f^0 = -393.5 \text{ kJ/mol}$$
for $H_2O(g)$,
$$\Delta H_f^0 = -241.8 \text{ kJ/mol}$$
for $CO(g)$,
$$\Delta H_f^0 = -110.5 \text{ kJ/mol}$$
Unknown: exothermic
or not

$\Delta H = \Delta H_f^0(\text{products}) - \Delta H_f^0(\text{reactants})$

$= 1 \text{ mol}(-241.8 \text{ kJ/mol}) + 2 \text{ mol}(-110.5 \text{ kJ/mol}) -$
$1 \text{ mol}(-109 \text{ kJ/mol}) - 1 \text{ mol}(-393.5 \text{ kJ/mol})$

$= 39.5 \text{ kJ}$

ΔH is positive, so the reaction is not exothermic.

45. Given:
for $NO_2(g)$,
$$\Delta H_f^0 = 33.1 \text{ kJ/mol}$$
for $N_2O_4(g)$,
$$\Delta H_f^0 = 9.1 \text{ kJ/mol}$$
Unknown: ΔH

$2NO_2(g) \rightarrow N_2O_4(g)$

$\Delta H = \Delta H_f^0(\text{products}) - \Delta H_f^0(\text{reactants})$

$= 1 \text{ mol}(9.1 \text{ kJ/mol}) - 2 \text{ mol}(33.1 \text{ kJ/mol})$

$= -57.1 \text{ kJ/mol}$

50. Given:
$$S(s) + \tfrac{3}{2}O_2(g) \rightarrow SO_3(g),$$
$$\Delta H = -395.8 \text{ kJ}$$
$$2SO_2(g) + O_2(g) \rightarrow$$
$$2SO_3(g), \Delta H = -198.2 \text{ kJ}$$
Unknown: ΔH_f^0 for $SO_2(g)$

$\tfrac{1}{2}[2SO_2(g) + O_2(g) \rightarrow 2SO_3(g), \Delta H = -198.2 \text{ kJ}]$
$SO_2(g) + \tfrac{1}{2}O_2(g) \rightarrow SO_3(g), \Delta H = -99.1 \text{ kJ}$

$S(s) + \tfrac{3}{2}O_2(g) \rightarrow \cancel{SO_3(g)}$	$\Delta H = -395.8 \text{ kJ}$
$\cancel{SO_3(g)} \rightarrow SO_2(g) + \tfrac{1}{2}O_2(g)$	$\Delta H = 99.1 \text{ kJ}$
$S(s) + O_2(g) \rightarrow SO_2(g)$	$\Delta H = -296.7 \text{ kJ}$

51. Given:
for $HCl(g)$,
$$\Delta G_f^0 = -92.307 \text{ kJ/mol}$$
for $H_2(g)$ and $Cl_2(g)$,
$$\Delta G_f^0 = 0 \text{ kJ/mol}$$
$$H_2(g) + Cl_2(g) \rightarrow 2HCl(g)$$
Unknown: ΔG, spontaneous or not

$\Delta G = \Delta G_f^0(\text{products}) - \Delta G_f^0(\text{reactants})$

$= 2 \text{ mol}(-92.307 \text{ kJ/mol}) - 1 \text{ mol}(0 \text{ kJ/mol}) - 1 \text{ mol}(0 \text{ kJ/mol})$

$= -184.614 \text{ kJ}$

ΔG is negative, so the reaction is spontaneous.

52. Given:
$$6CO_2(g) + 6H_2O(l) \rightarrow$$
$$C_6H_{12}O_6(s) + 6O_2(g)$$
$$\Delta H = 2870 \text{ kJ}$$
$$\Delta S = 259 \text{ J/K}$$
$$T = 297 \text{ K}$$
Unknown: ΔG

$\Delta G = \Delta H - T\Delta S$

$= 2870 \text{ kJ} - (297 \text{ K})(0.259 \text{ kJ/K})$

$= 2790 \text{ kJ}$

Solutions Manual *continued*

53. Given:

Reaction 1: $\Delta H = 125$ kJ
$T = 293$ K
$\Delta S = 35$ J/K
Reaction 2: $\Delta H = -85.2$ kJ
$T = 127$ K
$\Delta S = 125$ J/K
Reaction 3: $\Delta H = -275$ kJ
$T = 500°C$
$= 773$ K
$\Delta S = 45$ J/K

Unknown: ΔG, spontaneous or not

$\Delta G = \Delta H - T\Delta S$

Reaction 1: $\Delta G = 125$ kJ $- (293$ K$)(0.035$ kJ/K$)$

$= 115$ kJ

ΔG is positive, so it is not spontaneous.

Reaction 2: $\Delta G = -85.2$ kJ $- (127$ K$)(0.125$ J/K$)$

$= -101$ kJ

ΔG is negative, so it is spontaneous.

Reaction 3: $\Delta G = -275$ kJ $- (773$ K$)(0.045$ kJ/K$)$

$= -3.1 \times 10^2$ kJ

ΔG is negative, so it is spontaneous.

54. Given:

$2H_2O(l) \rightarrow 2H_2(g) + O_2(g)$
$2HCl(g) \rightarrow H_2(g) + Cl_2(g)$
for $H_2O(l)$,
$\Delta H_f^0 = -285.8$ kJ/mol,
$\Delta S^0 = 70.0$ J/K $\bullet$ mol
for $H_2(g)$,
$\Delta H_f^0 = 0$ kJ/mol,
$\Delta S^0 = 130.7$ J/K $\bullet$ mol
for $O_2(g)$,
$\Delta H_f^0 = 0$ kJ/mol,
$\Delta S^0 = 205.1$ J/K $\bullet$ mol
for $HCl(g)$,
$\Delta H_f^0 = -92.3$ kJ/mol,
$\Delta S^0 = 186.9$ J/K $\bullet$ mol
for $Cl_2(g)$,
$\Delta H_f^0 = 0$ kJ/mol,
$\Delta S^0 = 223.1$ J/K $\bullet$ mol
$T = 25°C = 298$ K

Unknown: spontaneous or not

$\Delta H = \Delta H_f^0(\text{products}) - \Delta H_f^0(\text{reactants})$

$\Delta S = \Delta S(\text{products}) - \Delta S_f^0(\text{reactants})$

$\Delta G = \Delta H - T\Delta S$

for $2H_2O(l) \rightarrow 2H_2(g) + O_2(g)$:

$\Delta H = 2$ mol$(0$ kJ/mol$) + 1$ mol$(0$ kJ/mol$) - 2$ mol$(-285.8$ kJ/mol$)$

$= 571.6$ kJ

$\Delta S = 2$ mol$(130.7$ J/K $\bullet$ mol$) + 1$ mol$(205.1$ J/K $\bullet$ mol$) -$
2 mol$(70.0$ J/K $\bullet$ mol$)$

$= 326.6$ J/K

$\Delta G = 571.6$ kJ $- (298$ K$)(0.3266$ J/K$)$

$= 474.3$ kJ

not spontaneous

for $2HCl(g) \rightarrow H_2(g) + Cl_2(g)$:

$\Delta H = 1$ mol$(0$ kJ/mol$) + 1$ mol$(0$ kJ/mol$) - 2$ mol$(-95.3$ kJ/mol$)$

$= 190.6$ kJ

$\Delta S = 1$ mol$(130.7$ J/K $\bullet$ mol$) + 1$ mol$(223.1$ J/K $\bullet$ mol$) -$
2 mol$(186.9$ J/K $\bullet$ mol$)$

$= -2.00 \times 10^1$ J/K

$\Delta G = 1.85 \times 10^2$ kJ $- (298$ K$)(-0.0200$ kJ/K$)$

$= 196$ kJ

not spontaneous

Solutions Manual *continued*

55. Given:
NH$_4$NO$_3$(s) →
  NH$_4$NO$_3$(aq, 1 m)
for NH$_4$NO$_3$(s),
  ΔS^0 = 151.1 J/K • mol
for NH$_4$NO$_3$(aq, 1 m),
  ΔS^0 = 259.8 J/K • mol

Unknown: ΔS

$\Delta S = \Delta S^0$(products) − ΔS^0(reactants)

= 1 mol(259.8 J/K • mol) − 1 mol(151.1 J/K • mol)

= 108.7 J/K

70. Given: y_2 = 3.3 K
  y_1 = 5.6 K
  x_2 = 50 s
  x_1 = 30 s

Unknown: slope

slope = $\dfrac{\Delta y}{\Delta x}$

$= \dfrac{3.3 \text{ K} - 5.6 \text{ K}}{50 \text{ s} - 30 \text{ s}}$

= −0.1 K/s

71. Given: y_2 = 63.7 mL
  y_1 = 43.5 mL
  x_2 = 5 s
  x_1 = 2 s

Unknown: slope

slope = $\dfrac{\Delta y}{\Delta x}$

$= \dfrac{63.7 \text{ mL} - 43.5 \text{ mL}}{5 \text{ s} - 2 \text{ s}}$

= 7 mL/s

Standardized Test Prep

10. Given:
C(s) + 2H$_2$(g) → CH$_4$(g)
for C(s) + O$_2$(g) → CO$_2$(g),
  ΔH = −393 kJ
for 2H$_2$(g) + O$_2$(g) →
  2H$_2$O(l),
  ΔH = −572 kJ
for CH$_4$(g) + 2O$_2$(g) →
  CO$_2$(g) + 2H$_2$O(l),
  ΔH = −891 kJ

Unknown: ΔH

C(s) + O$_2$(g) → CO$_2$(g) $\quad \Delta H$ = −393 kJ

2H$_2$(g) + O$_2$(g) → 2H$_2$O(l) $\quad \Delta H$ = −572 kJ

CO$_2$(g) + 2H$_2$O(l) → CH$_4$(g) + 2O$_2$(g) $\quad \Delta H$ = 891 kJ

C(s) + 2H$_2$(g) → CH$_4$(g) $\quad \Delta H$ = −74 kJ

Problem Bank

1. Given: CH$_4$ ΔH =
  −890 kJ/mol
  m = 3.2 g

Unknown: ΔH

$(3.2 \text{ g CH}_4)\left(\dfrac{\text{mol CH}_4}{16 \text{ g CH}_4}\right) = 0.2 \text{ mol CH}_4$

(0.2 mol)(−890 kJ/mol) = −180 kJ

2. Given: m = 55 g
  ΔT = 94.6°C −
  22.4°C
  = 72.2°C
  c_p of aluminum =
  0.897 J/(g•K)

Unknown: q

$c_p = \dfrac{q}{m \times \Delta T}$

$q = c_p \times m \times \Delta T$

= (0.897 J/(g•K))(55 g)(72.2°C)

= 3600 J

Solutions Manual *continued*

3. Given: $q = 3500$ J
$m = 28.2$ g
$T_i = 20°C$
$\quad = 293$ K

Unknown: T_f

c_p of iron $= 0.449$ J/(g$\cdot$K)

$$c_p = \frac{q}{m \times \Delta T}$$

$$\Delta T = \frac{q}{m \times c_p}$$

$$= \frac{3500 \text{ J}}{(28.2 \text{ g})(0.449 \text{ J/(g}\cdot\text{K)})}$$

$$= 276.422 \text{ K}$$

$$\Delta T = T_f - T_i$$

$$T_f = \Delta T + T_i$$

$$= 276.422 \text{ K} + 293 \text{ K}$$

$$= 570 \text{ K}$$

---

4. Given: $CH_4(g) + 2O_2(g) \rightarrow CO_2(g) + H_2O(l)$

Unknown: ΔH for combustion of CH_4

$CH_4(g) \rightarrow C(s) + 2H_2(g)$
$\Delta H_f^0 = 74.9$ kJ/mol

$C(s) + O_2(g) \rightarrow CO_2$
$\Delta H_f^0 = -393.5$ kJ/mol

$2H_2(g) + O_2 \rightarrow 2H_2O(l)$
$\Delta H_f^0 = 2(-285.8 \text{ kJ/mol})$

$$= -571.6 \text{ kJ/mol}$$

$CH_4(g) + 2O_2 \rightarrow CO_2(g) + H_2O(l)$
$\Delta H^0 = -890.2$ kJ/mol

Total energy produced

$$= -(-890.2 \text{ kJ/mol}) \times 1 \text{ mol}$$

$$= 890.2 \text{ kJ}$$

Solutions Manual *continued*

5. Given: $2N_2(g) + 5O_2(g) \rightarrow 2N_2O_5(g)$

Unknown: ΔH

$$2H_2O(l) \rightarrow 2H_2(g) + 2\left(\frac{1}{2}O_2\right)(g)$$

$\Delta H_f^0 = 2(285.8 \text{ kJ/mol})$

$\qquad = 571.6 \text{ kJ/mol}$

$(2)2NHO_3(l) \rightarrow 2N_2O_5(g) + 2H_2O(l)$

$\Delta H^0 = 2(76.6 \text{ kJ/mol})$

$\qquad = 153.2 \text{ kJ/mol}$

$$(4)\frac{1}{2}N_2(g) + (4)\frac{3}{2}O_2(g) + (4)\frac{1}{2}H_2(g) \rightarrow 4HNO_3(l)$$

$\Delta H_f^0 = 4(-174.1 \text{ kJ/mol})$

$\qquad = -696.4 \text{ kJ/mol}$

Solution:

$2N_2(g) + 5O_2(g) \longrightarrow 2N_2O_5(g)$

$\Delta H = 28.4 \text{ kJ/mol}$

---

6. Unknown: ΔH_f of butane (C_4H_{10})

Balanced equations:

$4C(s) + 5H_2(g) \rightarrow C_4H_{10}(g)$

$4C(s) + 4O_2(g) \rightarrow 4CO_2(g)$

$\Delta H = 4(-393.5 \text{ kJ/mol})$

$\qquad = -1574 \text{ kJ/mol}$

$$5H_2(g) + \frac{5}{2}O_2(g) \rightarrow 5H_2O(l)$$

$\Delta H = 5(-285.8 \text{ kJ/mol})$

$\qquad = -1429 \text{ kJ/mol}$

$$4CO_2(g) + 5H_2O \rightarrow C_4H_{10}(g) + \frac{13}{2}O_2(g)$$

$\Delta H^0 = 2877.6 \text{ kJ/mol}$

Solution:

$4C(s) + 5H_2(g) \rightarrow C_4H_{10}(g)$

$\Delta H = -125.4 \text{ kJ/mol}$

Solutions Manual *continued*

7. Unknown: ΔH_c of 1 mol of N_2 to form NO_2

Balanced equation:

$$N_2(g) + 2O_2(g) \rightarrow 2NO_2(g)$$

$$\tfrac{1}{2}N_2(g) + O_2 \rightarrow NO_2(g)$$

$$\Delta H_f^0 = 33.2 \text{ kJ/mol}$$

$$(2)\tfrac{1}{2}N_2(g) + (2)O_2(g) \rightarrow (2)NO_2(g)$$

$$\Delta H = 2(33.2 \text{ kJ/mol})$$

$$= 66.4 \text{ kJ/mol}$$

For 1 mol N_2, the heat of combustion is (66.4 kJ/mol) $\times$ (1 mol) = 66.4 kJ

8. Unknown: ΔH_f of SO_2 from S and O

Balanced equation:

$$S(s) + O_2(g) \rightarrow SO_2(g)$$

$$S(s) + \tfrac{3}{2}O_2 \rightarrow SO_3(g)$$

$$\Delta H = -395.2 \text{ kJ/mol}$$

$$\left(\tfrac{1}{2}\right)2SO_3(g) \rightarrow \left(\tfrac{1}{2}\right)2SO_2(g) + \left(\tfrac{1}{2}\right)O_2(g)$$

$$\Delta H_0 = \left(\tfrac{1}{2}\right)(-(-198.2 \text{ kJ/mol}))$$

$$= 99.1 \text{ kJ/mol}$$

$$S(s) + O_2(g) \rightarrow SO_2(g)$$

$$\Delta H = -296.1 \text{ kJ/mol}$$

For 1 mol sulfur dioxide, the energy required is $-(-296.1$ kJ/mol) $\times$ (1 mol) = 296.1 kJ

Solutions Manual *continued*

9. a. Given: $CaCO_3(s) \rightarrow CaO(s) + CO_2(g)$

$$CaCO_3(s) \rightarrow Ca(s) + C(s) + \frac{3}{2}O_2(g)$$

$$\Delta H = 1206.9 \text{ kJ/mol}$$

$$Ca(s) + \frac{1}{2}O_2(g) \rightarrow CaO(s)$$

$$\Delta H = -634.9 \text{ kJ/mol}$$

$$C(s) + O_2(g) \rightarrow CO_2(g)$$

$$\Delta H = -393.51 \text{ kJ/mol}$$

Solution:

$$CaCO_3(s) \rightarrow CaO(s) + CO_2(g)$$

$$\Delta H = 178.49 \text{ kJ/mol}$$

$\Delta H = [\text{sum of } \Delta H_f \text{ of products}] - [\text{sum of } \Delta H_f \text{ of reactants}]$

$\Delta H = [H_f^0 CaO + \Delta H_f^0 CO_2]$

$\quad - [\Delta H_f^0 CaCO_3]$

$\quad = [(-634.9 \text{ kJ/mol})$

$\quad\quad + (-393.51 \text{ kJ/mol})]$

$\quad\quad - (-1206.9 \text{ kJ/mol})$

$\quad\quad = 178.49 \text{ kJ/mol}$

b. Given: $Ca(OH)_2(s) \rightarrow CaO(s) + H_2O(g)$

$$Ca(OH)_2(s) \rightarrow Ca(s) + O_2(g) + H_2(g)$$

$$\Delta H = 983.2 \text{ kJ/mol}$$

$$Ca(s) + \frac{1}{2}O_2(g) \rightarrow CaO(s)$$

$$\Delta H = -634.9 \text{ kJ/mol}$$

$$H_2(g) + \frac{1}{2}O_2(g) \rightarrow H_2O(g)$$

$$\Delta H = -241.8 \text{ kJ/mol}$$

Solution:

$$Ca(OH)_2(s) \rightarrow CaO(s) + H_2O(g)$$

$$\Delta H = 106.5 \text{ kJ/mol}$$

$\Delta H = [\Delta H_f^0 CaO + \Delta H_f^0 H_2O]$

$\quad - [\Delta H_f^0 CaCO_3]$

$\quad = [(-634.9 \text{ kJ/mol})$

$\quad\quad + (-241.8 \text{ kJ/mol})]$

$\quad\quad - (-983.2 \text{ kJ/mol})$

$\quad\quad = 106.5 \text{ kJ/mol}$

Solutions Manual *continued*

c. Given:
$$Fe_2O_3(s) + 3CO(g) \rightarrow 2Fe(s) + 3CO_2(g)$$

$$Fe_2O_3(s) \rightarrow 2Fe(s) + \frac{3}{2}O_2(g)$$

$$\Delta H = 825.5 \text{ kJ/mol}$$

$$3CO(g) \rightarrow 3C(s) + \frac{3}{2}O_2(g)$$

$$\Delta H = 3(110.5 \text{ kJ/mol})$$

$$= 331.5 \text{ kJ/mol}$$

$$3C(s) + 3O_2(g) \rightarrow 3CO_2(g)$$

$$\Delta H = 3(-393.5 \text{ kJ/mol})$$

$$= -1180.5 \text{ kJ/mol}$$

Solution:

$$Fe_2O_3(s) + 3CO(g) \rightarrow 2Fe(s) + 3CO_2(g)$$

$$\Delta H = -23.5 \text{ kJ/mol}$$

$$\Delta H = [2\Delta H_f^0 Fe + 3\Delta H_f^0 CO_2]$$

$$- [\Delta H_f^0 Fe_2O_3 + 3\Delta H_f^0 CO]$$

$$= [0 + 3(-393.5 \text{ kJ/mol})]$$

$$- [(825.5 \text{ kJ/mol})$$

$$+ 3(110.5 \text{ kJ/mol})]$$

$$= -23.5 \text{ kJ/mol}$$

---

10. a. Unknown: ΔH

$$C_2H_6(g) + \frac{7}{2}O_2(g) \rightarrow 2CO_2(g) + 3H_2O(l)$$

$$C_2H_6(g) \rightarrow 2C(s) + 3H_2(g)$$

$$\Delta H = 83.8 \text{ kJ/mol}$$

$$2C(s) + 2O_2(g) \rightarrow 2CO_2(g)$$

$$\Delta H = 2(-393.5 \text{ kJ/mol}) = -787 \text{ kJ/mol}$$

$$3H_2(g) + \frac{3}{2}O_2(g) \rightarrow 3H_2O(l)$$

$$\Delta H = 3(-285.8 \text{ kJ/mol}) = -857.4 \text{ kJ/mol}$$

Solution:

$$C_2H_6(g) + \frac{7}{2}O_2(g) \rightarrow 2CO_2(g) + 3H_2O(l)$$

$$\Delta H = [2\Delta H_f^0 CO_2 + 3\Delta H_f^0 H_2O]$$

$$- [\Delta H_f^0 C_2H_6 + \frac{7}{2}\Delta H_f^0 O_2]$$

$$= [2(-393.5 \text{ kJ/mol})$$

$$+ 3(-285.8 \text{ kJ/mol})]$$

$$- [(-83.8 \text{ kJ/mol}) - 0]$$

$$= -1560 \text{ kJ/mol}$$

Solutions Manual   **S-21**   Causes of Change

Solutions Manual *continued*

b. Unknown: ΔH

$$C_6H_6(g) + \frac{15}{2}O_2(g) \rightarrow 6CO_2(g) + 3H_2O(l)$$

$$C_6H_6(l) \rightarrow 6C(s) + 3H_2(g)$$

$$\Delta H = -49.08 \text{ kJ/mol}$$

$$6C(s) + 6O_2(g) \rightarrow 6CO_2(g)$$

$$\Delta H = 6(-393.5 \text{ kJ/mol}) = -2361 \text{ kJ/mol}$$

$$3H_2(g) + \frac{3}{2}O_2(g) \rightarrow 3H_2O(l)$$

$$\Delta H = 3(-285.8 \text{ kJ/mol}) = -857.4 \text{ kJ/mol}$$

Solution:

$$C_6H_6(g) + \frac{15}{2}O_2(g) \rightarrow 6CO_2(g) + 3H_2O(l)$$

$$\Delta H = [6\Delta H_f^0 CO_2 + 3\Delta H_f^0 H_2O]$$

$$- [\Delta H_f^0 C_2H_6 + \frac{15}{2}\Delta H_f^0 O_2]$$

$$= [6(-393.5 \text{ kJ/mol})$$

$$+ 3(-285.8 \text{ kJ/mol})]$$

$$- [(-49.08 \text{ kJ/mol}) - 0]$$

$$= -3267 \text{ kJ/mol}$$

11. Given: ΔH_f^0 of $C_2H_5OH =$ −277 kJ/mol

Unknown: ΔH of C_2H_5OH

Balanced equation:

$$C_2H_5OH(l) + 3O_2(g) \rightarrow 2CO_2(g) + 3H_2O(l)$$

$$C_2H_5OH \rightarrow 2C + 3H_2 + \frac{1}{2}O_2$$

$$\Delta H = -(-277 \text{ kJ/mol})$$

$$2C + 2O_2 \rightarrow 2CO_2$$

$$\Delta H = 2(-393.5 \text{ kJ/mol}) = (-787 \text{ kJ/mol})$$

$$3H_2 + \frac{3}{2}O_2 \rightarrow 3H_2O$$

$$\Delta H = 3(-285.8 \text{ kJ/mol}) = -857.4 \text{ kJ/mol}$$

Solution:

$$C_2H_5OH(l) + 3O_2(g) \rightarrow 2CO_2(g) + 3H_2O(l)$$

$$\Delta H = -1367 \text{ kJ/mol}$$

Solutions Manual *continued*

12. Given: ΔH_f^0 for $SO_2 =$ -0.2968 kJ/(mol·K)

Unknown: ΔH_f^0 for 30 g SO_2

$(30 \text{ g } SO_2)\left(\dfrac{\text{mol } SO_2}{64.1 \text{ g } SO_2}\right) = 0.468019 \text{ mol } SO_2$

$(0.468019 \text{ mol } SO_2)(0.2968 \text{ kJ/(mol·K)}) = 0.14 \text{ kJ}$

---

13. a. Unknown: Sign of ΔS^0

$CaCO_3(s) \rightarrow CaO(s) + CO_2(g)$

1 mol $\rightarrow$ 2 mol

ΔS^0 increases; $\Delta S^0 > 0 (+\Delta S^0)$

b. Unknown: Sign of ΔS^0

$2SO_2(g) + O_2(g) \rightarrow 2SO_3(g)$

3 mol $\rightarrow$ 2 mol

ΔS^0 decreases; $\Delta S^0 < 0 (-\Delta S^0)$

---

14. Given: $Cu_2S(s) + S(s) \rightarrow 2CuS(s)$

$\Delta H = -26.7$ kJ/mol

$\Delta S = -0.0197$ kJ/(mol·K)

$T = 298$ K

Unknown: ΔG; Whether reaction will be spontaneous?

$\Delta G = \Delta H - T\Delta S$

$= -26.7$ kJ/mol

$\quad - (298 \text{ K})(-(-0.0197 \text{ kJ/(mol·K)}))$

$= -26.7$ kJ/mol $- (-5.8706$ kJ/mol$)$

$= -20.8$ kJ/mol

---

15. Yes; reaction will be spontaneous (ΔG^0 is negative).

---

16. 1. Unknown: whether ΔS_0 will be $> 0, < 0$ or $= 0$

1. $3H_2(g) + N_2(g) \rightarrow 2NH_3(g)$

4 mol(g) $\rightarrow$ 2 mol(g)

S^0 decreases; $\Delta S^0 < 0$

2. $2Mg(s) + O_2(g) \rightarrow 2MgO(s)$

2. $2Mg(s) + O_2(g) \rightarrow 2MgO(s)$

3 mol $\rightarrow$ 2 mol

S^0 decreases; $\Delta S^0 < 0$

3. $C_6H_{12}O_6(s) + 6O_2(g) \rightarrow 6CO_2(g) + 6H_2O(g)$

3. $C_6H_{12}O_6(s) + 6O_2(g) \rightarrow 6CO_2(g) + 6H_2O(g)$

7 mol $\rightarrow$ 12 mol

S^0 increases; $\Delta S^0 > 0$

4. $KNO_3(s) \rightarrow K^+(aq) + NO_3^-(aq)$

4. $KNO_3(s) \rightarrow K^+(aq) + NO_3^-(aq)$

1 mol $\rightarrow$ 2 mol

S^0 increases; $\Delta S^0 > 0$

Solutions Manual Causes of Change

Solutions Manual *continued*

17. a. Given: $\Delta H = 125$ kJ/mol

Unknown: ΔG; whether reaction will occur spontaneously

$T = 293$ K

$\Delta S = 0.035$ kJ/(mol•K)

$\Delta G = \Delta H - T\Delta S$

$= (125 \text{ kJ/mol})$

$\quad - (293 \text{ K})(0.035 \text{ kJ/(mol•K)})$

$= 114.745$ kJ/mol

Not spontaneous

b. Given: $\Delta H = -85.2$ kJ/mol

Unknown: ΔG; whether reaction will occur spontaneously

$T = 400$ K

$\Delta S = 0.125$ kJ/(mol•K)

$\Delta G = \Delta H - T\Delta S$

$= (-85.2 \text{ kJ/mol})$

$\quad - (400 \text{ K})(0.035 \text{ kJ/(mol•K)})$

$= -135.2$ kJ/mol

Spontaneous

c. Given: $\Delta H = -275$ kJ/mol

Unknown: ΔG; whether reaction will occur spontaneously

$T = 773$ K

$\Delta S = 0.45$ kJ/(mol•K)

$\Delta G = \Delta H - T\Delta S$

$= (-275 \text{ kJ/mol})$

$\quad - (773 \text{ K})(0.45 \text{ kJ/(mol•K)})$

$= -622.85$ kJ/mol

Spontaneous

18. a. Given: $C(s) + O_2(g) \rightarrow CO_2(g) + 393.51$ kJ/mol
$\Delta S^0 = 0.003$ kJ/(mol•K)
$T = 298.15$ K

Unknown: ΔG^0

$\Delta G = \Delta H - T\Delta S$

$\Delta H = -393.51$ kJ/mol

$\Delta G = (-393.51 \text{ kJ/mol})$

$\quad - (298.15 \text{ K})(0.003 \text{ kJ/(mol•K)})$

$= -394.404$ kJ/mol $= 400$ kJ/mol

b.

$\Delta G < 0$, spontaneous

19. Given: Temperature $= 300K$
$\Delta H = -74.8$ kJ/mol
$\Delta S = -0.0809$ kJ/(mol•K)

Unknown: if reaction will occur spontaneously

$\Delta G = \Delta H - T\Delta S$

$= (-74.8 \text{ kJ/mol})$

$\quad - (300K)(-0.0809 \text{ kJ/(mol•K)})$

$= -50.53$ kJ/mol

yes, it will occur spontaneously.

Solutions Manual *continued*

20. Given: $T = 298.15$ K

$Fe_2O_3(s) + 2Al\ (s) \rightarrow$
$2Fe\ (s) + Al_2O_3(s)$
$\Delta H^0 =$
-851.5 kJ/mol
$\Delta S^0 = -0.0385$ kJ/
$(mol \cdot K)$

Unknown: ΔG at 448 K

$\Delta G = \Delta H - T\Delta S$

$= (-851.5$ kJ/mol$)$

$- (448$ K$)(-0.0385$ kJ/$(mol \cdot K))$

$= -834.252$ kJ/mol

---

21. Given: $4FeO(s) + O_2(g) \rightarrow$
$2Fe_2O_3(s)$

Unknown: The change in enthalpy

$(4)FeO(s) \rightarrow (4)Fe(s) + (4)O_2(g)$

$\Delta H = 4(272$ kJ/mol$)$

$= 1088$ kJ/mol

$(2)2Fe(s) + (2)\dfrac{3}{2}O_2(g) \rightarrow (2)Fe_2O_3(s)$

$\Delta H = 2(-824.2$ kJ/mol$)$

$= -1648.4$ kJ/mol

$4FeO(s) + O_2(g) \rightarrow 2Fe_2O_3(s)$

$\Delta H = -560$ kJ/mol